THE Plant Based Diet

COOKBOOK for beginners

The Complete Step-by-Step Guide to Lose Weight & Energize Your Body, Including a Weekly Meal Plan and Fresh & Easy Recipes for Novice and Busy People

COPYRIGHT - 2021 -

ALL RIGHTS RESERVED.

The content contained within this book may not be reproduced, duplicated or transmitted without direct written permission from the author or the publisher. Under no circumstances will any blame or legal responsibility be held against the publisher, or author, for any damages, reparation, or monetary loss due to the information contained within this book. Either directly or indirectly.

LEGAL NOTICE:

This book is copyright protected. This book is only for personal use. You cannot amend, distribute, sell, use, quote or paraphrase any part, or the content within this book, without the consent of the author or publisher.

DISCLAIMER NOTICE:

Please note the information contained within this document is for educational and entertainment purposes only. All effort has been executed to present accurate, up to date, and reliable, complete information. No warranties of any kind are declared or implied. Readers acknowledge that the author is not engaging in the rendering of legal, financial, medical or professional advice. The content within this book has been derived from various sources. Please consult a licensed professional before attempting any techniques outlined in this book.

By reading this document, the reader agrees that under no circumstances is the author responsible for any losses, direct or indirect, which are incurred as a result of the use of information contained within this document, including, but not limited to, - errors, omissions, or inaccuracies.

TABLE OF CONTENTS

INTRODUCTION 9

CHAPTER 1
Features and Benefits of the
Plant-Based Diet 11

CHAPTER 2
Differences Between a Vegetarian/
Vegan Diet and a Plant-Based Diet 15

CHAPTER 3
What Should You Eat and
What Should You Avoid? 19

CHAPTER 4
A Week Meal Plan 27

CHAPTER 5
Breakfast Recipes 29
- Grapes and Green Smoothie 30
- Kale and Mango Smoothie 31
- Pomegranate Smoothie 32
- Coconut Water Smoothie 33
- Apple, Banana and Berry Smoothie 34
- Ginger Berry Zing Smoothie 35
- Dragon Fruit Smoothie Bowl 36
- Chocolate Smoothie Bowl 37
- Zucchini and Blueberry Smoothie 38
- Pink and Hot Beet Smoothie 39
- Flour and Chickpea Frittata 40
- Potato Pancakes 41
- Chocolate Chip Pancakes 42
- Turmeric Steel-Cut Oats 43
- Vegetable Pancakes 44
- Banana and Chia Pudding 45
- Tofu Scramble 46
- Pumpkin Spice Oatmeal 47
- Peanut Butter Bites 48
- Cinnamon and Maple Overnight Oats 49

CHAPTER 6
Mains Recipes 51
- Black Bean Burgers 52
- Dijon Maple Burgers 53
- Hearty Black Lentil Curry 54
- Flavorful Refried Beans 55
- Smoky Red Beans and Rice 56
- Spicy Black-Eyed Peas 57
- Creamy Artichoke Soup 58
- Super Radish Avocado Salad 59

- Beauty School Ginger Cucumbers — 60
- Mushroom Salad — 61
- Red Quinoa and Black Bean Soup — 62
- October Potato Soup — 63
- Rice with Asparagus and Cauliflower — 64
- Spaghetti and Tomato Sauce — 65
- Crispy Cauliflower florets — 66
- Avocado Bread with Chickpeas — 67
- Onion Soup — 68
- Potato Soup — 69
- Teriyaki Eggplant — 70
- Broccoli Stir-Fry with Sesame Seeds — 71
- Tomato-Braised Lentils — 72
- Caesar White Bean Burgers — 73
- Quinoa Stuffed Peppers — 74
- Tofu Chickpea Stir-Fry — 75
- Smoky Burrito Tempeh — 76
- Sweet and Sour Tempeh — 77
- Korean Braised Tofu — 78
- Red Lentil Tikka Masala — 79
- Thai Red Tofu Curry — 80
- Barbecue Baked Seitan Strips — 81
- Teriyaki Glazed Tofu Steaks — 82
- Chili Sin Carne — 83
- Teriyaki Tofu Stir-Fry — 84
- Farro Protein Bowl — 85
- Mongolian Seitan — 86
- Black Bean and Quinoa Balls — 87
- Teriyaki Tempeh Tacos — 88
- Spinach Ricotta Lasagna — 89
- Samosa Pie — 90
- Lentil Roast with Balsamic Onion Gravy — 91

CHAPTER 7

Salads Recipes — 93
- Arugula with Fruits and Nuts — 94
- Broccoli Salad — 95
- Brunoise Salad — 96
- Brussels Sprouts and Ricotta Salad — 97
- Celery and Raisins Snack Salad — 98
- Dijon Celery Salad — 99
- Fresh Endive Salad — 100
- Fresh Salad with Orange Dressing — 101
- Greek Salad Skewers — 102
- Moroccan Leeks Snack Salad — 103
- Beans Snack Salad — 104
- Rainbow Salad — 105
- Roasted Butternut and Chickpeas Salad — 106
- Salad with Cranberries and Apple — 107
- Sirt Fruit Salad — 108
- Sprouts and Apples Snack Salad — 109
- Tomato and Avocado Salad — 110
- Avocado-Potato Salad — 111

- Avocado with Raspberry Vinegar Salad — 112
- Bitter Greens, Sprouts, Avocado and Orange Salad — 113

CHAPTER 8
Soups and Stews Recipes — 115
- Cannellini Bean Soup with Kale — 116
- Coconut Watercress Soup — 117
- Easy Borscht — 118
- Potato and Corn Chowder — 119
- Pumpkin Soup — 120
- Cannellini Pesto Spaghetti — 121
- Classic Tomato Soup — 122
- Minestrone Soup — 123
- Scallion and Mint Soup — 124
- Green Pea Soup — 125
- Kale and Lentils Stew — 126
- Lentil Soup with Swiss Chard — 127
- Spicy Farro Soup — 128
- Chickpea Noodle Soup — 129
- Greens and Grains Soup — 130
- Vegan Pho — 131
- Creamy Spinach Rotini Soup — 132
- Hot and Sour Tofu Soup — 133
- Winter Quinoa Soup — 134

CHAPTER 9
Pasta and Noodles Recipes — 135
- Stir-Fry Noodles — 136
- Spicy Sweet Chili Veggie Noodles — 137
- Creamy Vegan Mushroom Pasta — 138
- Vegan Chinese Noodles — 139
- Vegetable Penne Pasta — 140
- Spaghetti in Spicy Tomato Sauce — 141
- 20 Minutes Vegetarian Pasta — 142
- Creamy Vegan Pumpkin Pasta — 143
- Loaded Creamy Vegan Pesto Pasta — 144
- Creamy Vegan Spinach Pasta — 145

CHAPTER 10
Homemade Sauces and Condiments Recipes — 147
- Catalina Dressing — 148
- Coleslaw Dressing — 149
- Walnut Basil Dressing — 150
- Moroccan Carrot Dip — 151
- Tahini Citrus Dressing — 152
- Curried Almond Dressing — 153
- Applesauce Salad Dressing — 154
- Balsamic Vinaigrette — 155
- Chipotle Lime Dressing — 156
- White Beans Dip — 157
- Edamame Hummus — 158
- Beans Mayonnaise — 159
- Cashew Cream — 160

- Lemon Tahini 161
- Keto-Vegan Ketchup 162
- Avocado Hummus 163
- Guacamole 164
- Keto-Vegan Mayo 165
- Peanut Sauce 166
- Pistachio Dip 167

- ## CHAPTER 11
  Rice and Grains Recipes 169
- Classic Garlicky Rice 170
- Brown Rice with Vegetables and Tofu 171
- Basic Amaranth Porridge 172
- Country Cornbread with Spinach 173
- Rice Pudding with Currants 174
- Millet Porridge with Sultanas 175
- Quinoa Porridge with Dried Figs 176
- Bread Pudding with Raisins 177
- Bulgur Wheat Salad 178
- Rye Porridge with Blueberry Topping 179
- Coconut Sorghum Porridge 180
- Dad's Aromatic Rice 181
- Everyday Savory Grits 182
- Greek-Style Barley Salad 183
- Easy Sweet Maize Meal Porridge 184
- Mom's Millet Muffins 185
- Ginger Brown Rice 186
- Sweet Oatmeal "Grits" 187
- Freekeh Bowl with Dried Figs 188
- Cornmeal Porridge with Maple Syrup 189

CHAPTER 12
Smoothies and Beverages Recipes 191
- Max Power Smoothie 192
- Chai Chia Smoothie 193
- Trope-Kale Breeze 194
- Hydration Station 195
- Mango Madness 196
- Chocolate PB Smoothie 197
- Pink Panther Smoothie 198
- Banana Nut Smoothie 199
- Light Ginger Tea 200
- Kale Smoothie 201
- Hot Tropical Smoothie 202
- Berry Smoothie 203
- Cranberry and Banana Smoothie 204
- Pumpkin Smoothie 205
- Super Smoothie 206
- Kiwi and Strawberry Smoothie 207
- Banana and Chai Chia Smoothie 208
- Chocolate and Peanut Butter Smoothie 209
- Golden Milk 210
- Mango Agua Fresca 211

CHAPTER 13
Snacks Recipes — 213
- Cinnamon and Hemp Seed Coffee Shake — 214
- Green Smoothie — 215
- Strawberry and Banana Smoothie — 216
- Orange Smoothie — 217
- Pumpkin Chai Smoothie — 218
- Banana Shake — 219
- Green Honeydew Smoothie — 220
- Summer Salsa — 221
- Red Salsa — 222
- Pinto Bean Dip — 223
- Smoky Red Pepper Hummus — 224
- Spinach Dip — 225
- Tomatillo Salsa — 226
- Arugula Pesto Couscous — 227
- Oatmeal and Raisin Balls — 228
- Nacho Cheese — 229
- Pico de Gallo — 230
- Beet Balls — 231
- Cheesy Crackers — 232
- Tomato Soup — 233

CHAPTER 14
Desserts Recipes — 235
- Raspberry Muffins — 236
- Chocolate Chip Cake — 237
- Coffee Cake — 238
- Chocolate Marble Cake — 239
- Chocolate Chip Cookies — 240
- Lemon Cake — 241
- Banana Muffins — 242
- No-Bake Cookies — 243
- Peanut Butter and Oats Bars — 244
- Baked Apples — 245
- Chocolate Strawberry Shake — 246
- Chocolate Clusters — 247
- Banana Coconut Cookies — 248
- Chocolate Pots — 249
- Maple Syrup and Tahini Fudge — 250
- Creaseless — 251
- Peanut Butter, Nut and Fruit Cookies — 252
- Chocolate Covered Dates — 253
- Vanilla Hot Chocolate — 254
- Vanilla Cupcakes — 255

CONCLUSION — 257

INTRODUCTION

WHAT DOES PLANT-BASED DIET MEAN?

A Plant-Based Diet includes eating whole plant foods. The diet restricts the intake of animal-based food and fat. Whole plant foods are rich in carbohydrates and fiber, which helps in keeping your body fit. This type of diet is very popular in most parts of the world as they supply all necessary nutrients, vitamins and minerals to the body.

WHY A PLANT-BASED DIET?

A plant-based diet is healthy for the body. It controls blood pressure and cholesterol level. Here are some health benefits it provides to the body:

- This diet is rich in carbohydrates and fiber. It helps in weight loss and has positive effects on diabetes as it keeps blood sugar under control. Eating a lot of fruits and vegetables retains your body fit. It controls high blood pressure, cholesterol and other heart diseases as you will be eating whole grains, vegetables, legumes and fresh fruits which are low in fat. By following this type of diet, you will be boosting your energy levels as plant-based foods are filled with vitamins, minerals and protein, which is necessary for your body to function properly.

- It provides instant energy as plant-based foods are rich in complex carbohydrates and fiber that release glucose slowly in the bloodstream. A plant-based diet is low in fat. It lets you eat as much food as you need without gaining weight. A plant-based diet improves liver function and prevents diseases such as inflammation and cirrhosis of the liver.

- You can build muscles by consuming plant-based foods which are loaded with proteins like quinoa, soybeans, tofu, legumes, etc. Protein helps in muscle recovery after strenuous exercises. Foods such as legumes, whole grains, nuts and seeds are a great source of proteins whereas fruits and vegetables provide vitamins to your body.

- This diet prevents the risk of diabetes, heart disease and cancer. Plant-based foods are low in calories and cholesterol. It keeps blood sugar levels stable and controls diabetes.

- A plant-based diet helps in lowering cholesterol levels as it is made up of complex carbohydrates. It prevents heart disease as it controls cholesterol levels. A plant-based diet helps to regulate blood sugar levels as all foods are low in fat. By following this diet, you will be preventing the risk of cancer as most plant-based foods are rich in antioxidants, which help to fight against free radical damage that can lead to cancer.

People today are health conscious, and most of them usually follow a strict diet to keep their bodies healthy and fit. A plant-based diet is one of the most popular diets as it provides tons of health benefits to your body. The food items in a plant-based diet are low in calories, sugar, fat, sodium, saturated fat and cholesterol but high in fiber, complex carbohydrates. Fruits and vegetables have fewer calories than other types of food items. Many people choose to follow vegan diets or vegetarian diets because they believe it gives them more energy and they feel healthier too.

This book is about a plant-based diet and recipes that you can try out. It will provide you with complete information about plant-based diets and recipes for healthy eating.

CHAPTER 1

FEATURES AND BENEFITS OF THE PLANT-BASED DIET

There are many benefits to follow this diet, mainly an overall increase in wellness and being less sick. The concept has been around for a long time that increasing consumption of plant-derived foods makes the person more active and healthier. These people also seem to be happier and less irritated, which makes life easier and far more relaxing. Other advantages which come with the diet are:

- There's no need to count calories in this diet: It can be a tedious and time-wasting task that a busy person cannot afford. This diet simply allows some food and restricts the rest. A calorie doesn't talk much about the food, what nutrients are in it, or if it is healthy or not.

- It is a good way to lose weight: A recent 2018 control experiment showed that people that follow a vegan diet, rather than those who eat meat, were more likely to lose weight. The study followed obese participants following normal diets and some following vegan diets, and the result was that vegan dieters almost lost 15 pounds in 4 months.

- Plant-based foods are full of carbs and fiber, which fills up the stomach quickly, making you feel less hungry. You will consume less of the foods that will be no good for you, like sodas or candies. Cravings will not hit you as hard as if you were hungry.

- There is a higher quantity of water in plant-based food which increases body metabolism and reduces appetite. Water has many benefits, being hydrated makes you have better hair, skin and makes you look fresh.

- Eating mostly plant-based foods decreases mortality by preventing lifelong diseases. A recent 2019 test by the American Heart Association showed that plant-based food eaters were less likely to develop heart diseases. It is also linked with lowering the chances of stroke, diabetes type 2, hypertension and obesity.

- It also increase insulin sensitivity in patients with diabetes. In the 2009 study, over tens of thousands of participants were approached and the percentage of vegans developing diabetes was found to be 2.9% less than others. A study published in 2018 stated that diabetes is improved when following any diet that increases plant content.

This diet doesn't require any sort of investment, and a person can begin it as soon as they decide to. Plant-based products are everywhere and even in a normal diet, take a big portion of it. Some dieting programs and fads take a lot of money from people giving only temporary results, but this diet has shown to reduce the most amount of weight.

For some people starting this diet can be hard, but if you want to reach your weight loss goals or become fit, this diet is suited for you.

THE MAIN BENEFITS OF A PLANT-BASED NUTRITION

1. Lowers cholesterol: Becoming environmentally friendly can significantly bring down the measure of LDL cholesterol in your blood, the awful kind that can prompt coronary illness and stroke. Maintain a strategic distance from margarine, cut out greasy meats and settle on plant-based nourishments. Dairy and industrial products contain fat and have no fiber. Plant-based diets contain no cholesterol at all. That implies veggie lover sustenance is vastly improved for your heart and your wellbeing.

2. Lowers blood pressure: At the point when you eat greasy meats and dairy items, the consistency of your blood increments, setting more weight on the veins. A plant-based diet tops you off with veggies and natural products, which are high in potassium. The higher intake of potassium balances blood thickness. This is the reason veggie lovers and vegetarians will, in general, have lower paces of hypertension, "the quiet executioner," as per observational examinations distributed in the Nutrition Review.

3. Prevents cancer: High-fat weight control plans have been connected to higher paces of malignant growth. In the plant-based diet, instead, fiber assumes an essential job in keeping your stomach-related framework spotless and solid, expelling disease-causing mixes before they can make hurt. A veggie lover diet and vegetarian diet are high in fiber, low in soaked and trans-fats and regularly incorporate a more organic product, vegetables and other malignancy averting phytochemicals.

4. Prevents heart disease: Research has discovered that a regular, low-fat, plant-based diet can help diminish cholesterol, lose weight and lower pulse. All of this causes heart problems.

5. Maintains healthy weight and fitness: The individuals who pursue a plant-based, veggie lover or vegan diet, for the most part, devour fewer calories and have lower body loads than the individuals who don't, as indicated by the Mayo Clinic. A plant-based diet doesn't ensure weight reduction. You'll need to keep your admission of desserts and greasy nourishments low, pick entire grains, eat an assortment of foods grown from the ground, and pick without fat and low-fat dairy items. Additionally, recall that cooking strategy tallies. Steam, bubble, flame broil or meal as opposed to fry.

STEP-BY-STEP INSTRUCTIONS TO TRANSITION TO A PLANT-BASED DIET

Aside from merely maintaining a strategic distance from meat, there are approaches to facilitate the change to a principally plant-based diet. Increment the measure of grains, products of the soil on your plate bit by bit until the meat is the littlest bit of your supper. An online vegetarian conveyance administration can make the procedure basic.

Chapter 2

Differences Between a Vegetarian/Vegan Diet and a Plant-Based Diet

Vegan, vegetarian and plant-based diets are very similar (because they are based on vegetables) but also have different characteristics.

VEGETARIAN

Officially, the vegetarian diet has existed since around 700 B.C. However, this is not really true since human physiology clearly shows that we developed as omnivores (i.e., we ate whatever we could find). As collecting plants is easier and less risky than hunting, people lived on this for most of the year. Once technology improved and the first animals were domesticated, meat became easier to come by, and the human population exploded.

Today, people choose to adopt a vegetarian diet for many reasons, e.g.: ethics, religion, environmentalism, health, etc. A vegetarian diet's essence is to refrain from poultry, beef, game, fish, shellfish, or any by-products of animals. However, while vegetarians do not eat meat, most of them use animal-derived products, e.g.: fur, leather or wool.

There are several types of a vegetarian diet, the most common ones of which are:

- Lacto-ovo vegetarian: The followers of this diet avoid all meat but consume dairy and eggs.

- Lacto vegetarian: They refrain from meat and eggs but use dairy.

- Ovo vegetarian: These are vegetarians who avoid meat and dairy but use eggs.

- Pescatarians: They don't consume meat or poultry but eat fish.

- Flexitarians: These are people who can be qualified as part-time vegetarians i.e., they refrain from meat and fish from time to time.

VEGAN

This type of diet became popular relatively recently, although many people practice it out of necessity, i.e., when they can't get hold of eggs, dairy, meat, fish, etc. Some believe that veganism is more of a philosophy than a diet. It is based on the idea that the only way not to contribute to animal cruelty is to stay away from all animal products, i.e.: meat, poultry, fish, shellfish, dairy, eggs, honey, leather, fur, wool, etc. This is a very healthy diet but needs to be very carefully planned so you don't become nutrient-deficient as some essential nutrients are found only in animal-based foods.

PLANT-BASED DIET

A plant-based diet consists mainly of plants, fruits and vegetables, but does not exclude the use of meat and fish, although these are usually taken only occasionally. There are many variations of this diet, and they are generally considered an extremely healthy way of eating.

However, a plant-based diet can also be very unhealthy if it is based on plant-based foods but also includes refined grains and plant-based junk foods, e.g.: sugary beverages, sweets, high-starch foods, etc. So, a plant-based diet is only healthy if it is based on whole grains, healthy fats and healthy protein.

Besides, on a plant-only diet (this is different from a plant-based diet), it's even more important to focus on high-quality foods.

TIPS AND PLANT-BASED SUBSTITUTIONS

Many people do not want to try out a plant-based diet because they think they have to give up on their delicious meat, animal products and other juicy (but unhealthy) foodstuffs. This is only half true. They do have to give up on unhealthy food, but that does not mean they cannot enjoy delicious foods ever again.

Chapter 3

What Should You Eat and What Should You Avoid?

What Foods to Eat?

STARCH-FREE VEGETABLES

- Eggplant.
- Zucchini.
- Herbs (rosemary, basil,...).
- Broccoli.
- Tomatoes.

STARCHY VEGETABLES

- All kinds of potatoes.
- Whole corn.
- Legumes (all beans and lentils).
- Root vegetables.
- Quinoa.

FRUITS
- All fruits.

WHOLE GRAINS
- Whole brown rice and oats.

SPICES
- All spices.

BEVERAGES
- Water.
- Green tea.
- Unsweetened plant-based milk.
- Decaffeinated coffee and tea.

OMEGA-3 SOURCES
- Chia seeds.
- Ground flaxseed.
- Almonds.
- Nuts.
- Peanuts.
- Walnuts.
- Cashews.

In the move to an herbal diet, people should concentrate on consuming the following food groups:

FRUITS

- Avocado.
- Berries.
- Bananas.
- Citrus fruits.
- Apples.
- Melons.
- Grapes.

VEGETABLES

There are plenty of vegetables in a balanced diet focused on plants. A wide range of vitamins and minerals is available with a variety of colorful vegetables. For example:

- Kale.
- Broccoli.
- Beetroot.
- Carrots.
- Cauliflower.
- Asparagus.
- Peppers.
- Tomatoes.
- Zucchini.

Root vegetables are an essential source of vitamins and carbohydrates.

- Butternut squash.
- Sweet potato.
- Potatoes.
- Beets.

LEGUMES

Legumes are a healthy fiber and vegetable protein source. People may have a wide range of foods, including:

- Lentils.
- Chickpeas.
- Black beans.
- Peas.
- Kidney beans.

SEEDS

Semitic grains are an excellent snack or a simple way to add additional nutrients to a salad or soup. Sesame seeds are an excellent foundation of Vitamin E and calcium, as are sunflower seeds.

For example:

- Flax.
- Pumpkin.
- Hemp.
- Chia.

NUTS

- Cashews.
- Brazil.
- Almonds.
- Pecans.
- Pistachios.
- Macadamia.

HEALTHFUL FATS

Polyunsaturated, monounsaturated and omega-3 fatty acids are essential for consumption. Plant sources include:

- Hemp seeds.
- Avocados.
- Chia seeds.
- Walnuts.
- Canola oil.
- Flaxseed.
- Olive oil.

WHOLE GRAINS

They are a source of fiber and contribute to maintain steady blood sugar.

The whole grain examples include:

- Buckwheat.
- Brown rice.
- Oats.
- Quinoa.

- Rye.
- Whole grain bread.
- Barley.

PLANT-BASED MILK

In food and on-line, there is a wide variety of herbal dairy products available for people who want to reduce their milk consumption, including:

- Almond.
- Coconut.
- Soy.
- Oat.
- Rice.
- Hemp.

Just choose unsweetened milk options for plants.

WHAT FOODS TO AVOID?

Automatically reducing or replacing animal foods does not mean that a plant-based diet is healthy. You should also reduce or avoid unhealthy foods, such as:

PROCESSED FOODS

- White carbohydrates processed.
- Excess salt.
- Alternatives consisting of vegan and vegetarian salt and a lot of sugar.
- Seafood.
- Fatty, greasy, or deep-fried foods.
- Fish.
- Processed meat.
- Poultry.
- Red meat.

DAIRY

- Yogurt.
- Cream.
- Milk.
- Buttermilk.
- Cheese.

ADDED FATS

- Liquid oils.
- Margarine.
- Coconut oil.
- Butter.

BEVERAGES

- Fruit juice.
- Soda.
- Energy drinks.
- Sports drinks.
- Blended coffee and tea drinks.

VEGAN FOODS

- Vegan "cheese" and vegan "meat".

MISCELLANEOUS

- Pastries.
- Eggs.
- Candy bars.
- Energy bars.
- Cookies.
- Cakes.

Chapter 4

A Week Meal Plan

	BREAKFAST	LUNCH	DINNER	SNACK
SUNDAY	Grapes and Green Tea Smoothie	Black Bean Burger	Tomato-Braised Lentils	Raspberry Muffins
MONDAY	Chickpea Flour Frittata	Hearty Black Lentil Curry	Quinoa Stuffed Peppers	Cinnamon and Hemp Seed Coffee Shake
TUESDAY	Dragon Fruit Smoothie Bowl	Flavorful Refried Beans	Tofu Chickpea Stir-Fry	Coffee Cake
WEDNESDAY	Potato Pancakes	Spaghetti with Tomato Sauce	Barbecue Baked Seitan Strips	Pico de Gallo
THURSDAY	Chocolate Chip Pancake	Smoky Red Beans and Rice	Chili Sin Carne	Lemon Cake
FRIDAY	Mango and Kale Smoothie	Crispy Cauliflower	Teriyaki Tofu Stir Fry	Cheesy Crackers
SATURDAY	Peanut Butter Bites	Broccoli Stir-Fry with Sesame Seeds	Farro Protein Bowl	Arugula Pesto Couscous

Chapter 5

Breakfast Recipes

Grapes and Green Smoothie

PREPARATION TIME
5'

COOK TIME
0'

SERVING
2

NUTRITION

Calories: 150
Fat: 2.5g
Protein: 1g
Carbs: 36.5g
Fiber: 9g

INGREDIENTS

½ cup green tea
½ cup of green grapes
1 banana, peeled
1-inch piece of ginger
½ cup of ice cubes
2 cups baby spinach
½ of a medium apple, peeled, diced

DIRECTIONS

1. Place all the ingredients into the jar of a high-speed food processor or blender in the order stated in the ingredients list, and then cover it with the lid.
2. Pulse for 1 minute until smooth and then serve.

Kale and Mango Smoothie

PREPARATION TIME
5'

COOK TIME
0'

SERVING
2

NUTRITION

Calories: 281
Fat: 3g
Protein: 6g
Carbs: 63g
Fiber: 16g

INGREDIENTS

2 cups oats milk, unsweetened
2 bananas, peeled
½ cup kale leaves
2 teaspoons coconut sugar
1 cup mango pieces
1 teaspoon vanilla extract, unsweetened

DIRECTIONS

1. Place all the ingredients into the jar of a high-speed food processor or blender in the order stated in the ingredients list, and then cover it with the lid.
2. Pulse for 1 minute until smooth and then serve.

Pomegranate Smoothie

PREPARATION TIME
5'

COOK TIME
0'

SERVING
2

NUTRITION

Calories: 141.5
Fat: 1.1g
Protein: 4.1g
Carbs: 30.8g
Fiber: 2.4g

INGREDIENTS

2 cups almond milk, unsweetened
2 medium apples, cored, sliced
2 bananas, peeled
2 cups frozen raspberries
1 cup pomegranate seeds
4 teaspoons agave syrup

DIRECTIONS

1. Place all the ingredients into the jar of a high-speed food processor or blender in the order stated in the ingredients list, and then cover it with the lid.
2. Pulse for 1 minute until smooth and then serve.

Coconut Water Smoothie

INGREDIENTS

2 cups of coconut water
1 large apple, peeled, cored, diced
1 cup of frozen mango pieces
2 teaspoons peanut butter
4 teaspoons coconut flakes

PREPARATION TIME
5'

COOK TIME
0'

SERVING
2

DIRECTIONS

1. Place all the ingredients into the jar of a high-speed food processor or blender in the order stated in the ingredients list, and then cover it with the lid.
2. Pulse for 1 minute until smooth and then serve.

NUTRITION

Calories: 113.4
Fat: 0.3g
Protein: 0.6g
Carbs: 29g
Fiber: 2g

Apple, Banana and Berry Smoothie

PREPARATION TIME
5'

COOK TIME
0'

SERVING
2

NUTRITION

Calories: 156.1
Fat: 3.2g
Protein: 3g
Carbs: 17g
Fiber: 5.8g

INGREDIENTS

2 cups almond milk, unsweetened
2 cups frozen strawberries
2 bananas, peeled
1 large apple, peeled, cored, diced
2 tablespoons peanut butter

DIRECTIONS

1. Place all the ingredients into the jar of a high-speed food processor or blender in the order stated in the ingredients list, and then cover it with the lid.
2. Pulse for 1 minute until smooth and then serve.

Ginger Berry Zing Smoothie

PREPARATION TIME
5'

COOK TIME
0'

SERVING
2

NUTRITION

Calories: 300
Fat: 8g
Protein: 8g
Carbs: 30g
Fiber: 9g

INGREDIENTS

2 cups almond milk, unsweetened
1 cup frozen raspberries
1 cup of frozen strawberries
1 cup cauliflower florets
1-inch pieces of ginger

DIRECTIONS

1. Place all the ingredients into the jar of a high-speed food processor or blender in the order stated in the ingredients list, and then cover it with the lid.
2. Pulse for 1 minute until smooth and then serve.

Dragon Fruit Smoothie Bowl

PREPARATION TIME
5'

COOK TIME
0'

SERVING
2

NUTRITION

Calories: 225
Fat: 1.6g
Protein: 8.1g
Carbs: 48g
Fiber: 8.9g

INGREDIENTS

FOR THE BOWL:
½ cup coconut milk, unsweetened
2 bananas, peeled
½ cup frozen raspberries
7 ounces frozen dragon fruit
3 tablespoons vanilla protein powder

FOR THE TOPPINGS:
1 tablespoon coconut flakes
2 tablespoons hemp seeds

DIRECTIONS

1. Place all the ingredients for the bowl into the jar of a high-speed food processor or blender in the order stated in the ingredients list, and then cover it with the lid.
2. Pulse for 1 minute until smooth and then divide evenly between two bowls.
3. Sprinkle 1 tablespoon of coconut flakes and hemp seeds over the smoothie and then serve.

Chocolate Smoothie Bowl

PREPARATION TIME
5'

COOK TIME
0'

SERVING
2

NUTRITION

Calories: 382
Fat: 14g
Protein: 22g
Carbs: 53g
Fiber: 9g

INGREDIENTS

FOR THE BOWLS:
2 cups almond milk, unsweetened
2 bananas, peeled
3 tablespoons cocoa powder
1 cup spinach leaves, fresh
2 tablespoons oat flour
4 Medjool dates, pitted
1/8 teaspoon salt
2 tablespoons vanilla protein powder
2 tablespoons peanut butter

FOR THE TOPPINGS:
1 tablespoon coconut flakes
2 tablespoons hemp seeds

DIRECTIONS

1. Place all the ingredients for the bowl into the jar of a high-speed food processor or blender in the order stated in the ingredients list, and then cover it with the lid.
2. Pulse for 1 minute until smooth and then divide evenly between two bowls.
3. Sprinkle 1 tablespoon of coconut flakes and hemp seeds over the smoothie and then serve

Zucchini and Blueberry Smoothie

PREPARATION TIME
5'

COOK TIME
0'

SERVING
2

NUTRITION

Calories: 218
Fat: 10.1g
Protein: 6.3g
Carbs: 31.8g
Fiber: 4.7g

INGREDIENTS

1 cup coconut milk, unsweetened
1 large celery stem
2 bananas, peeled
1/2 cup spinach leaves, fresh
1 cup frozen blueberries
2/3 cup sliced zucchini
1 tablespoon hemp seeds
1/2 teaspoon maca powder
1/4 teaspoon ground cinnamon

DIRECTIONS

1. Place all the ingredients into the jar of a high-speed food processor or blender in the order stated in the ingredients list, and then cover it with the lid.
2. Pulse for 1 minute until smooth and then serve.

Pink and Hot Beet Smoothie

PREPARATION TIME
5'

COOK TIME
0'

SERVING
2

NUTRITION

Calories: 260.8
Fat: 1.3g
Protein: 13g
Carbs: 56g
Fiber: 9.3g

INGREDIENTS

2 cups almond milk, unsweetened
2 clementine, peeled
1 cup raspberries
1 banana, peeled
1 medium beet, peeled, chopped
2 tablespoons chia seeds
1/8 teaspoon sea salt
1/2 teaspoon vanilla extract, unsweetened
4 tablespoons almond butter

DIRECTIONS

1. Place all the ingredients into the jar of a high-speed food processor or blender in the order stated in the ingredients list, and then cover it with the lid.
2. Pulse for 1 minute until smooth and then serve.

Flour and Chickpea Frittata

PREPARATION TIME
10'

COOK TIME
50'

SERVING
6

NUTRITION

Calories: 153
Fat: 4g
Protein: 7g
Carbs: 20g
Fiber: 4g

INGREDIENTS

1 medium green bell pepper, cored, chopped
1 cup chopped greens
1 cup cauliflower florets, chopped
½ cup chopped broccoli florets
½ of a medium red onion, peeled, chopped
¼ teaspoon salt
½ cup chopped zucchini

FOR THE BATTER:
¼ cup cashew cream
½ cup chickpea flour
½ cup chopped cilantro
½ teaspoon salt
¼ teaspoon cayenne pepper
½ teaspoon dried dill
¼ teaspoon ground black pepper
¼ teaspoon dried thyme
½ teaspoon ground turmeric
1 tablespoon olive oil
1 ½ cup water

DIRECTIONS

1. Switch on the oven, then set it to 375°F and let it preheat.
2. Take a 9-inch pie pan, grease it with oil, and then set aside until required.
3. Take a large bowl, place all the vegetables in it, sprinkle with salt and then toss until combined.
4. Prepare the batter and for this, add all the ingredients in it except for thyme, dill and cilantro and then pulse until combined and smooth.
5. Pour the batter over the vegetables, add dill, thyme and cilantro and then stir until combined.
6. Spoon the mixture into the prepared pan, spread evenly and then bake for 45 to 50 minutes until done and inserted toothpick into frittata comes out clean.
7. When it's done, let the frittata rest for about 10 minutes, cut it into slices and then serve.

POTATO PANCAKES

INGREDIENTS

½ cup white whole-wheat flour
3 large potatoes, grated
½ of a medium white onion, peeled, grated
1 jalapeno, minced
2 green onions, chopped
1 tablespoon minced garlic
1 teaspoon salt
¼ teaspoon baking powder
¼ teaspoon ground pepper
4 tablespoons olive oil
2 tablespoons water

PREPARATION TIME
10'

COOK TIME
20'

SERVING
10

NUTRITION

Calories: 69
Fat: 1g
Protein: 2g
Carbs: 12g
Fiber: 1g

DIRECTIONS

1. Take a large bowl, place all the ingredients except for oil and then stir until well combined; stir in 1 to 2 tablespoons water if needed to mix the batter.
2. Take a large skillet pan, place this pan over medium-high heat, add 2 tablespoons of oil and then let it heat.
3. Scoop the pancake mixture in portions into the pan, shape each portion like a pancake and then cook for 5 to 7 minutes per side until pancakes turn golden brown and thoroughly cooked.
4. When done, transfer the pancakes to a plate, add more oil into the pan and then cook more pancakes in the same manner.
5. Serve straight away.

CHOCOLATE CHIP PANCAKES

INGREDIENTS

1 cup white whole-wheat flour
½ cup chocolate chips, vegan, unsweetened
1 tablespoon baking powder
¼ teaspoon salt
2 teaspoons coconut sugar
½ teaspoon vanilla extract, unsweetened
1 cup almond milk, unsweetened
2 tablespoons coconut butter, melted
2 tablespoons olive oil

PREPARATION TIME
5'

COOK TIME
10'

SERVING
6

NUTRITION

Calories: 172
Fat: 6g
Protein: 2.5g
Carbs: 28g
Fiber: 8g

DIRECTIONS

1. Take a large bowl, place all the ingredients except for oil and chocolate chips and then stir until well combined.
2. Add chocolate chips and then fold until just mixed.
3. Take a large skillet pan, place it over medium-high heat, add 1 tablespoon oil and then let it heat.
4. Scoop the pancake mixture in portions into the pan, shape each portion like a pancake and then cook for 5 to 7 minutes per side until pancakes turn golden brown and thoroughly cooked.
5. When done, transfer the pancakes to a plate, add more oil into the pan and then cook more pancakes in the same manner.
6. Serve straight away.

Turmeric Steel-Cut Oats

PREPARATION TIME
5'

COOK TIME
10'

SERVING
2

NUTRITION

Calories: 234
Fat: 4g
Protein: 7g
Carbs: 41g
Fiber: 5g

INGREDIENTS

1/2 cup steel-cut oats
1/8 teaspoon salt
2 tablespoons maple syrup
1/2 teaspoon ground cinnamon
1/3 teaspoon turmeric powder
1/4 teaspoon ground cardamom
1/4 teaspoon olive oil
1/2 cups water
1 cup almond milk, unsweetened

FOR THE TOPPING:
2 tablespoons pumpkin seeds
2 tablespoons chia seeds

DIRECTIONS

1. Take a medium saucepan, place it over medium heat, add oats and then cook for 2 minutes until toasted.
2. Pour in the milk and water, stir until mixed and then bring the oats to a boil.
3. Then switch heat to medium-low level, simmer the oats for 10 minutes and add salt, maple syrup and all spices.
4. Stir until combined, cook the oats for 7 minutes or more until cooked to the desired level and when done, let the oats rest for 15 minutes.
5. When done, divide oats evenly between two bowls, top with pumpkin seeds and chia seeds and then serve.

Vegetable Pancakes

PREPARATION TIME
10'

COOK TIME
20'

SERVING
10

NUTRITION

Calories: 74
Fat: 0.3g
Protein: 3 g
Carbs: 16 g
Fiber: 2.7g

INGREDIENTS

1/3 cup cooked and mashed sweet potato
2 cups grated carrots
1 cup chopped coriander
1 cup cooked spinach
2 ounces chickpea flour
1/2 teaspoon baking powder
1 (1/2) teaspoon salt
1 teaspoon ground turmeric
2 tablespoons olive oil
3/4 cup of water

DIRECTIONS

1. Take a large bowl, place chickpea flour in it, add turmeric powder, baking powder and salt, and then stir until combined.
2. Whisk in the water until combined, stir in sweet potatoes until well mixed and then add carrots, spinach and coriander until well combined.
3. Take a large skillet pan, place it over medium-high heat, add 1 tablespoon oil and then let it heat.
4. Scoop the pancake mixture in portions into the pan, shape each portion like a pancake and then cook for 3 to 5 minutes per side until pancakes turn golden brown and thoroughly cooked.
5. When done, transfer the pancakes to a plate, add more oil into the pan and then cook more pancakes in the same manner.
6. Serve straight away.

Banana and Chia Pudding

PREPARATION TIME
25'

COOK TIME
12'

SERVING
2

NUTRITION

Calories: 495
Fat: 21g
Protein: 9g
Carbs: 76g
Fiber: 14g

INGREDIENTS

FOR THE PUDDING:
2 bananas, peeled
4 tablespoons chia seeds
2 tablespoons coconut sugar
1/2 teaspoon pumpkin pie spice
1/8 teaspoon sea salt
1/2 cup almond milk, unsweetened

FOR THE BANANAS:
2 bananas, peeled, sliced
1/8 teaspoon ground cinnamon
2 tablespoons coconut sugar
1/4 cup chopped walnuts
2 tablespoons almond milk, unsweetened

DIRECTIONS

1. Prepare the pudding and for this, place all the ingredients in a blender except for chia seeds and then pulse until smooth.
2. Pour the mixture into a medium saucepan, place this pan over medium heat, bring the mixture to a boil and then remove it from heat.
3. Add chia seeds into the hot banana mixture, stir until mixed and then let it sit for 5 minutes.
4. Whisk the pudding and then let it chill for 15 minutes in the refrigerator.
5. Meanwhile, prepare the caramelized bananas and for this, take a medium skillet pan and place it over medium heat.
6. Add banana slices, sprinkle with salt, coconut sugar and cinnamon, drizzle with milk and then cook for 5 minutes until the mixture has thickened.
7. Assemble the pudding and for this, divide the pudding evenly between two bowls, top with banana slices and sprinkle with walnuts and then serve.

Tofu Scramble

PREPARATION TIME
5'

COOK TIME
15'

SERVING
3

NUTRITION

Calories: 304
Fat: 25.6g
Protein: 14.2g
Carbs: 6.6g
Fiber: 2.6g

INGREDIENTS

12 ounces tofu, extra-firm, pressed, drained
½ of a medium red onion, peeled, sliced
1 cup baby greens mix
1 medium red bell pepper, cored, sliced
½ teaspoon garlic powder
1 teaspoon salt
½ teaspoon ground black pepper
¼ teaspoon turmeric powder
¼ teaspoon ground cumin
4 tablespoons olive oil, divided

DIRECTIONS

1. Take a large bowl, place tofu in it, and then break it into bite-size pieces.
2. Add salt, black pepper, turmeric and 2 tablespoons of oil, and then stir until mixed.
3. Take a medium skillet pan, place it over medium heat, add garlic powder and cumin and then cook for 1 minute until fragrant.
4. Add tofu mixture, stir until mixed, switch heat to medium-high level, and then cook for 5 minutes until tofu turn golden brown.
5. When done, divide tofu evenly between three plates, keep it warm, and then set aside until required.
6. Return the skillet pan over medium-high heat, add the remaining oil and let it heat until hot.
7. Add onion and bell peppers, cook for 5 to 7 minutes or until beginning to brown, and then season with a pinch of salt.
8. Add baby greens, toss until mixed, and then cook for 30 seconds until leaves begin to wilt.
9. Add vegetables evenly to the plates to the scrambled tofu and then serve.

Pumpkin Spice Oatmeal

PREPARATION TIME
5'

COOK TIME
8'

SERVING
2

NUTRITION

Calories: 175
Fat: 3.2g
Protein: 5.8g
Carbs: 33g
Fiber: 6.1g

INGREDIENTS

1/4 cup Medjool dates, pitted, chopped
2/3 cup rolled oats
1 tablespoon maple syrup
1/2 teaspoon pumpkin pie spice
1/2 teaspoon vanilla extract, unsweetened
1/3 cup pumpkin puree
2 tablespoons chopped pecans
1 cup almond milk, unsweetened

DIRECTIONS

1. Take a medium pot, place it over medium heat, and then add all the ingredients except for pecans and maple syrup.
2. Stir all the ingredients until combined and then cook for 5 minutes until the oatmeal has been absorbed all the liquid and thickened to the desired level.
3. When done, divide oatmeal evenly between two bowls, top with pecans and drizzle with maple syrup and then serve.

Peanut Butter Bites

PREPARATION TIME
10'

COOK TIME
0'

SERVING
5

NUTRITION

Calories: 103.1
Fat: 4.3g
Protein: 2.3g
Carbs: 15.4g
Fiber: 0.8g

INGREDIENTS

1 cup rolled oats
12 Medjool dates, pitted
½ cup peanut butter, sugar-free

DIRECTIONS

1. Plugin a blender or a food processor, add all the ingredients in its jar and then cover with the lid.
2. Pulse for 5 minutes until well combined and then tip the mixture into a shallow dish.
3. Shape the mixture into 20 balls, 1 tablespoon of mixture per ball, and then serve.

Cinnamon and Maple Overnight Oats

PREPARATION TIME
10'

COOK TIME
0'

SERVING
4

NUTRITION

Calories: 292
Fat: 9g
Protein: 7g
Carbs: 48g
Fiber: 6g

INGREDIENTS

2 cups almond milk, unsweetened
2 clementine, peeled
1 cup raspberries
1 banana, peeled
1 medium beet, peeled, chopped
2 tablespoons chia seeds
1/8 teaspoon sea salt
1/2 teaspoon vanilla extract, unsweetened
4 tablespoons almond butter

DIRECTIONS

1. Take four mason jars, and then add ½ cup oats, ¼ teaspoon vanilla and ½ cup milk in each jar.
2. Take a small bowl, add maple syrup, cinnamon and sugar, stir until mixed, add this mixture into the oats mixture and then stir until combined.
3. Cover the jars with the lid and then let them rest in the refrigerator for a minimum of 2 hours or more until thickened.
4. When ready to eat, top the oats with pecans, sprinkle with cinnamon, drizzle with maple syrup and then serve.

Chapter 6
Mains Recipes

Black Bean Burgers

INGREDIENTS

1 onion, diced
2 cloves garlic, minced
1/2 teaspoon oregano, dried
1/2 cup flour
1 jalapeno pepper, small
2 cups black beans, canned and mashed
1/4 cup breadcrumbs (vegan)
2 teaspoons parsley, minced
1/4 teaspoon cumin
1 tablespoon olive oil
2 teaspoons chili powder
1/2 red pepper, diced
Sea salt to taste

DIRECTIONS

1. Place the oil, flour, garlic, onion and oregano in a pan.
2. Cook over medium-high heat and then cook until the onions are translucent.
3. Stir in the peppers and sauté until tender, and then set it to the side.
4. Use a potato masher to mash your black beans, and then stir in the peppers, cumin, breadcrumbs, parsley, salt and chili powder, stir well and then divide it into six patties.
5. Cook until it's fried on each side and serve.

PREPARATION TIME
5'

COOK TIME
20'

SERVING
4

NUTRITION

Calories: 211
Carbs: 12g
Fat: 7g
Protein: 12g

Dijon Maple Burgers

PREPARATION TIME
10'

COOK TIME
40'

SERVING
12

NUTRITION

Calories: 209
Carbs: 11g
Fat: 5g
Protein: 9g

INGREDIENTS

1 red bell pepper
19 ounces chickpeas, rinsed and drained
1 cup almonds, ground
2 teaspoons Dijon mustard
1 teaspoon oregano
1/2 teaspoon sage
1 cup spinach, fresh
1 (1/2) cups rolled oats
1 clove garlic, pressed
1/2 lemon, juiced
2 teaspoons maple syrup, pure

DIRECTIONS

1. Get out a baking sheet. Line it with parchment paper.
2. Cut your red pepper in half and then take the seeds out. Place it on your baking sheet and roast in the oven while you prepare your other ingredients.
3. Process your chickpeas, almonds, mustard and maple syrup together in a food processor.
4. Add in your lemon juice, oregano, sage, garlic and spinach, processing again. Make sure it's combined, but don't puree it.
5. Once your red bell pepper is softened, which should roughly take 10 minutes, add this to the processor as well. Add in the oats, mixing well.

Hearty Black Lentil Curry

PREPARATION TIME
15'

COOK TIME
6 HOURS

SERVING
7

NUTRITION

Calories: 171
Carbs: 10g
Fat: 7g
Protein: 12g

INGREDIENTS

1 cup of black lentils, rinsed and soaked overnight
14 ounces of chopped tomatoes
2 large white onions, peeled and sliced
1 (1/2) teaspoons of garlic, minced
1 teaspoon of ginger, grated
1 red chili
1 teaspoon of salt
1/4 teaspoon of red chili powder
1 teaspoon of paprika
1 teaspoon of ground turmeric
2 teaspoons of ground cumin
2 teaspoons of ground coriander
4 ounces of vegetarian butter
1 fluid of ounce water
2 fluid of ounce vegetarian double cream

DIRECTIONS

1. Place a large pan over moderate heat, add butter and let heat until melted.
2. Add the onions, garlic and ginger and let cook for 10 to 15 minutes or until onions are caramelized.
3. Then stir in salt, red chili powder, paprika, turmeric, cumin, ground coriander and water.
4. Transfer this mixture to a 6-quart slow cooker, add tomatoes and red chili.
5. Drain lentils, add to slow cooker and stir until just mix.
6. Plug in the slow cooker; adjust cooking time to 6 hours and let cook on low heat setting.
7. When the lentils are done, stir in vegetarian cream and adjust the seasoning.
8. Serve with boiled rice or whole wheat bread.

Flavorful Refried Beans

INGREDIENTS

3 cups of pinto beans, rinsed
1 small jalapeno pepper, seeded and chopped
1 medium-sized white onion, peeled and sliced
2 tablespoons of minced garlic
5 teaspoons of salt
2 teaspoons of ground black pepper
1/4 teaspoon of ground cumin
9 cups of water

PREPARATION TIME
15'

COOK TIME
8 HOURS

SERVING
8

NUTRITION

Calories: 198
Carbs: 22g
Fat: 7g
Protein: 19g

DIRECTIONS

1. Using a 6-quart slow cooker, place all the ingredients and stir until it mixes properly.
2. Cover the top, plug in the slow cooker; adjust the cooking time to 6 hours, let it cook on a high heat setting and add more water if the beans get too dry.
3. When the beans are done, drain them and reserve the liquid.
4. Mash the beans using a potato masher and pour in the reserved cooking liquid until it reaches your desired mixture.
5. Serve immediately.

Smoky Red Beans and Rice

PREPARATION TIME
15'

COOK TIME
5 HOURS

SERVING
8

NUTRITION

Calories: 234
Carbs: 13g
Fat: 7g
Protein: 19g

INGREDIENTS

30 ounces of cooked red beans
1 cup of brown rice, uncooked
1 cup of chopped green pepper
1 cup of chopped celery
1 cup of white onion, chopped
1 1/2 teaspoons of garlic, minced
1/2 teaspoon of salt
1/4 teaspoon of cayenne pepper
1 teaspoon of paprika, smoked
2 teaspoons of dried thyme
1 bay leaf
2 1/3 cups of vegetable broth

DIRECTIONS

1. Using a 6-quart slow cooker, add all the ingredients there are except for the rice, salt and cayenne pepper.
2. Stir until it mixes appropriately and then cover the top.
3. Plug in the slow cooker; adjust the cooking time to 4 hours and steam on a low heat setting.
4. Then pour in and stir the rice, salt, cayenne pepper and continue cooking for an additional 2 hours at a high heat setting.

Spicy Black-Eyed Peas

PREPARATION TIME
15'

COOK TIME
60'

SERVING
8

NUTRITION

Calories: 211
Carbs: 22g
Fat: 7g
Protein: 19g

INGREDIENTS

32 ounces black-eyed peas, uncooked
1 cup of chopped orange bell pepper
8 ounces of chipotle peppers, chopped
1 cup of chopped carrot
1 cup of chopped white onion
1 teaspoon of minced garlic
3/4 teaspoon of salt
1 tablespoon of adobo sauce
2 tablespoons of olive oil
1 tablespoon of apple cider vinegar
4 cups of vegetable broth

DIRECTIONS

1. Place a medium-sized non-stick skillet pan over an average temperature of heat; add the bell peppers, carrot, onion, garlic, salt, oil and vinegar.
2. Stir until it mixes properly and let it cook for 5 to 8 minutes or until it gets translucent.
3. Transfer this mixture to a 6-quart slow cooker and add the peas, chipotle pepper, adobo sauce and vegetable broth.
4. Stir until mixed properly and cover the top.
5. Plug in the slow cooker; adjust the cooking time to 8 hours and let it cook on the low heat setting or until peas are soft.

CREAMY ARTICHOKE SOUP

PREPARATION TIME
5'

COOK TIME
40'

SERVING
4

NUTRITION

Calories: 211
Carbs: 12g
Fat: 7g
Protein: 11g

INGREDIENTS

1 can artichoke hearts, drained
3 cups vegetable broth
2 tablespoons lemon juice
1 small onion, finely cut
2 cloves garlic, crushed
3 tablespoons olive oil
2 tablespoons flour
1/2 cup vegan cream
A pinch of salt
A pinch of pepper

DIRECTIONS

1. Gently sauté the onion and garlic in some olive oil.
2. Add the flour, whisking constantly, and then add the hot vegetable broth slowly, while still whisking. Cook for about 5 minutes.
3. Blend the artichoke, lemon juice, salt and pepper until smooth. Add the puree to the broth mix, stir well and then stir in the cream.
4. Cook until heated through. Garnish with a swirl of vegan cream or a sliver of artichoke.

Super Radish Avocado Salad

PREPARATION TIME
10'

COOK TIME
25'

SERVING
2

NUTRITION

Calories: 211
Carbs: 9g
Fat: 7g
Protein: 12g

INGREDIENTS

6 shredded carrots
6 ounces diced radishes
1 diced avocado
1/3 cup ponzu

DIRECTIONS

1. Bring all the above ingredients together in a serving bowl and toss.
2. Enjoy!

Beauty School Ginger Cucumbers

PREPARATION TIME
10'

COOK TIME
5'

SERVING
2

NUTRITION

Calories: 210
Carbs: 14g
Fat: 7g
Protein: 19g

INGREDIENTS

1 sliced cucumber
3 teaspoons rice wine vinegar
1 (1/2) tablespoons sugar
1 teaspoon minced ginger

DIRECTIONS

1. Bring all the above ingredients together in a mixing bowl and toss the ingredients well.
2. Enjoy!

Mushroom Salad

PREPARATION TIME
10'

COOK TIME
20'

SERVING
2

NUTRITION

Calories: 191
Carbs: 6g
Fat: 7g
Protein: 17g

INGREDIENTS

1 tablespoon butter
½ pound cremini mushrooms, chopped
2 tablespoons Extra-virgin olive oil
Salt and black pepper to taste
2 bunches arugula
4 slices ham
1 tablespoon apple cider vinegar
4 sundried tomatoes in oil, drained and chopped
Fresh parsley leaves, chopped

DIRECTIONS

1. Heat a pan with butter and half of the oil.
2. Add the mushrooms, salt and pepper. Stir-fry for 3 minutes. Reduce heat. Stir again and cook for 3 minutes more.
3. Add the rest of the oil and vinegar. Stir and cook for 1 minute.
4. Place arugula on a platter, add ham on top, add the mushroom mixture, sundried tomatoes, more salt and pepper, parsley and serve.

Red Quinoa and Black Bean Soup

PREPARATION TIME
5'

COOK TIME
40'

SERVING
6

NUTRITION

Calories: 211
Carbs: 22g
Fat: 7g
Protein: 19g

INGREDIENTS

1/4 cup red quinoa
4 minced garlic cloves
1/2 tablespoon coconut oil
1 diced jalapeno
3 cups diced onion
2 teaspoons cumin
1 chopped sweet potato
1 teaspoon coriander
1 teaspoon chili powder
5 cups vegetable broth
15 ounces black beans
1/2 teaspoon cayenne pepper
2 cups spinach
2 cups water

DIRECTIONS

1. Begin by bringing the quinoa into a saucepan to boil with 2 cups of water. Allow the quinoa to simmer for 20 minutes. Next, remove the quinoa from heat.
2. To the side, heat onion, oil and garlic together in a large soup pot.
3. Add the jalapeno and the sweet potato and sauté for an additional 7 minutes.
4. Next, add all the spices and the broth and bring the soup to a simmer for 25 minutes. The potatoes should be soft.
5. Before serving, add the quinoa, black beans and spinach to the mix. Season and serve warm. Enjoy!

October Potato Soup

PREPARATION TIME
5′

COOK TIME
20′

SERVING
3

NUTRITION

Calories: 203
Carbs: 12g
Fat: 7g
Protein: 9g

INGREDIENTS

4 minced garlic cloves
2 teaspoons coconut oil
3 diced celery stalks
1 diced onion
2 teaspoons yellow mustard seeds
5 diced Yukon potatoes
6 cups vegetable broth
1 teaspoon oregano
1 teaspoon paprika
1/2 teaspoon cayenne pepper
1 teaspoon chili powder
Salt and pepper to taste

DIRECTIONS

1. Begin by sautéing the garlic and the mustard seeds together in the oil in a large soup pot.
2. Next, add the onion and sauté the mixture for another 5 minutes.
3. Add the celery, the broth, the potatoes and all the spices, and continue to stir.
4. Allow the soup to simmer for 30 minutes without a cover.
5. Next, position about three cups of the soup in a blender and puree the soup until you've reached a smooth consistency. Pour this back into the big soup pot, stir and serve warm. Enjoy!

Rice with Asparagus and Cauliflower

PREPARATION TIME
5'

COOK TIME
20'

SERVING
2

NUTRITION

Calories: 257
Carbs: 4g
Fat: 4g
Protein: 40g

INGREDIENTS

3 ounces asparagus
3 ounces cauliflower, chopped
2 ounces tomato sauce
1/2 cup of brown rice
3/4 cup of water
1/3 teaspoon salt
1/4 teaspoon ground black pepper
1/4 teaspoon garlic powder
1 tablespoon olive oil

DIRECTIONS

1. Take a medium saucepan, place it over medium heat and add oil, asparagus and cauliflower, and sauté for 5 to 7 minutes until golden brown.
2. Season with salt, garlic powder and black pepper, stir in tomato sauce and cook for 1 minute.
3. Add rice and pour in water, stir until mixed, cover with a lid and then cook for 10 to 12 minutes until rice has been absorbed all the liquid and become tender.
4. When done, remove the pan from heat and fluff the rice with a fork, then serve.

Spaghetti and Tomato Sauce

PREPARATION TIME
5'

COOK TIME
15'

SERVING
2

NUTRITION

Calories: 265
Carbs: 8g
Fat: 2g
Protein: 7g

INGREDIENTS

4 ounces spaghetti pasta
2 green onions, greens and whites separated
1/8 teaspoon coconut sugar
3 ounces tomato sauce
1 tablespoon olive oil
1/3 teaspoon salt
1/4 teaspoon ground black pepper

DIRECTIONS

1. Prepare the spaghetti pasta, and for this, cook it according to the directions on the packet, then set aside.
2. Then take a skillet pan, place it over medium heat and then add oil. When hot, add white parts of green onions and cook for 2 minutes until tender.
3. Add tomato sauce, season with salt and black pepper and then bring it to a boil.
4. Switch heat to medium-low level, simmer the sauce for 1 minute, and then add the cooked spaghetti and toss until mixed.
5. Divide the spaghetti between two plates and serve.

Crispy Cauliflower Florets

INGREDIENTS

6 ounces of cauliflower florets
1/2 of zucchini, sliced
1/2 teaspoon of sea salt
1/2 tablespoon curry powder
1/4 teaspoon maple syrup
2 tablespoons olive oil

PREPARATION TIME
5'

COOK TIME
15'

SERVING
2

NUTRITION

Calories: 161
Carbs: 2g
Fat: 2g
Protein: 7g

DIRECTIONS

1. Switch on the oven and set it to 450°F, let it preheat.
2. Meanwhile, take a medium bowl and add cauliflower florets and zucchini slices, add the remaining ingredients, reserving 1 tablespoon oil, toss until it's well coated.
3. Take a medium skillet pan, place it over medium-high heat and add the remaining oil, wait until it gets hot.
4. Spread cauliflower and zucchini in a single layer and sauté for 5 minutes, tossing frequently.
5. Then transfer the mixture to a baking sheet and put it into the oven, then bake for 8 to 10 minutes until vegetables have turned golden brown and thoroughly cooked, stirring halfway.

Avocado Bread with Chickpeas

PREPARATION TIME
5'

COOK TIME
5'

SERVING
2

NUTRITION

Calories: 235
Carbs: 5g
Fat: 5g
Protein: 31g

INGREDIENTS

1/2 of avocado, peeled, pitted
4 tablespoons canned chickpeas, liquid reserved
1 tablespoon lime juice
1 teaspoon apple cider vinegar
2 slices of bread, toasted
1/4 teaspoon salt
1/4 teaspoon paprika
1 teaspoon olive oil

DIRECTIONS

1. Take a medium skillet pan, place it over medium heat and add oil. When hot, add chickpeas and cook for 2 minutes.
2. Sprinkle paprika and salt over chickpeas, toss to coat and remove the pan from heat.
3. Place avocado in a bowl, mash by using a fork, drizzle with lime juice and vinegar, and stir until well mixed.
4. Spread mashed avocado over bread slices and scatter chickpeas on top, then serve.

Onion Soup

INGREDIENTS

6 green onions, chopped
7 ounces diced potatoes
1/3 teaspoon salt
2 tablespoons olive oil
1/4 cup vegetable broth
1/4 teaspoon ground white pepper
1/4 teaspoon ground coriander

PREPARATION TIME
5'

COOK TIME
12'

SERVING
2

NUTRITION

Calories: 191
Carbs: 1g
Fat: 1g
Protein: 15g

DIRECTIONS

1. Take a small pan, place potatoes in it and cover with water, then place the pan over medium heat.
2. Boil the potatoes until cooked and tender, and when done, drain the potatoes. Set aside until required.
3. Return saucepan over low heat, add oil and green onions and then cook for 5 minutes until cooked.
4. Season with pepper, salt and coriander, add potatoes, pour in vegetable broth, stir until mixed and bring it to simmer.
5. Remove the pan from heat and then blend the mixture by using an immersion blender until creamy.
6. Taste to adjust seasoning, ladle soup into bowls and serve.

Potato Soup

INGREDIENTS

2 potatoes, peeled, cubed
1/3 teaspoon salt
1/2 cup vegetable broth
3/4 cup of water
1/8 teaspoon ground black pepper
1 tablespoon Cajun seasoning

PREPARATION TIME
5'

COOK TIME
12'

SERVING
2

NUTRITION

Calories: 203
Carbs: 5g
Fat: 6g
Protein: 37g

DIRECTIONS

1. Take a small pan, place potato cubes in it and cover with water and vegetable broth, and then place the pan over medium heat.
2. Boil the potatoes until cooked and tender, and when done, remove the pan from heat, blend the mixture by using an immersion blender until creamy.
3. Return the pan over medium-low heat and add the remaining ingredients, stir until mixed and bring it to a simmer.
4. Taste to adjust seasoning, ladle soup into bowls and serve.

Teriyaki Eggplant

INGREDIENTS

1/2 pound eggplant
1 green onion, chopped
1/2 teaspoon grated ginger
1/2 teaspoon minced garlic
1/3 cup soy sauce
1 tablespoon coconut sugar
1/2 tablespoon apple cider vinegar
1 tablespoon olive oil

PREPARATION TIME
5'

COOK TIME
12'

SERVING
2

NUTRITION

Calories: 132
Carbs: 4g
Fat: 4g
Protein: 13g

DIRECTIONS

1. Prepare vegan Teriyaki sauce, and for this, take a medium bowl and add garlic, ginger, soy sauce, vinegar and sugar in it, then whisk until sugar has dissolved completely.
2. Cut eggplant into cubes, add them into vegan Teriyaki sauce and toss until well coated. Marinate for 10 minutes.
3. When ready to cook, take a grill pan and place it over medium-high heat, grease it with oil, and when hot, add marinated eggplant.
4. Cook for 3 to 4 minutes per side, until nicely browned and beginning to charred, drizzling with excess marinade frequently and then transfer to a plate.
5. Sprinkle green onion on top of the eggplant and serve.

Broccoli Stir-Fry with Sesame Seeds

PREPARATION TIME
10'

COOK TIME
8'

SERVING
4

NUTRITION

Calories: 135
Fat: 10.9g
Carbs: 9.7g
Protein: 4.1g
Fiber: 3.3g

INGREDIENTS

2 tablespoons extra-virgin olive oil
1 tablespoon grated fresh ginger
2 cups broccoli florets
¼ teaspoon sea salt (optional)
2 garlic cloves, minced
2 tablespoons toasted sesame seeds

DIRECTIONS

1. Heat the olive oil in a large nonstick skillet over medium-high heat until shimmering.
2. Fold in the ginger, broccoli and sea salt (if desired) and stir-fry for 5 to 7 minutes, or until the broccoli is browned.
3. Cook the garlic until tender, about 30 seconds.
4. Sprinkle with the sesame seeds and serve warm

Tomato-Braised Lentils

INGREDIENTS

1 garlic clove, sliced
4 tablespoons Extra virgin olive oil
1 bunch broccoli rabe
1 onion, chopped
1 tomato, chopped
1 garlic clove, minced
1/2 cup coconut cream
1/2 cup green French lentils
2 tablespoons plant-based butter
1 tablespoon tomato paste
3 cups vegetable stock
Salt and pepper to taste
1 handful fresh basil leaves, torn
Water
Ice

PREPARATION TIME
5'

COOK TIME
40'

SERVING
4

NUTRITION

Calories: 638
Fat: 32.6g
Total carbs: 63.2g
Protein: 28.6g

DIRECTIONS

1. Heat 2 tablespoons of olive oil in a saucepan over low heat, and then add in onions. Cook the onions until translucent and season with pepper and salt.
2. Add minced garlic to the pan and cook for 1 minute, then add in lentils, tomato paste and a splash of stock.
3. Turn the heat to medium and cook as you stir occasionally until the stock is absorbed. Add stock bit by bit as you stir occasionally for about 30 minutes until the lentils are tender.
4. In the meantime, prepare a large ice bath and bring another pot of water to boil. Add broccoli rabe into the pot with boiling water and cook for 1-2 minutes. Remove the broccoli rabe and place it into the ice bath.
5. Drain the cooled broccoli rabe and pat it dry. Heat the remaining 2 tablespoons of olive oil in a separate skillet, then add in sliced garlic clove and broccoli rabe. Season with pepper and salt and then sauté for about 2-3 minutes.
6. Add chopped tomato to lentils and cook for 2-3 minutes, then add in cream and butter. Stir in basil leaves and serve immediately. Enjoy with sautéed broccoli rabe on top.

Caesar White Bean Burgers

PREPARATION TIME
15'

COOK TIME
20'

SERVING
4

NUTRITION

Calories: 533
Fat: 13.7g
Total carbs: 76.8g
Protein: 26.7g

INGREDIENTS

2 garlic cloves, minced
2 tablespoons olive oil
1 flax egg
½ onion, diced
3 tablespoons lemon juice
2 cans (14 ounces) of white beans, drained and rinsed
¼ teaspoon salt
½ cup breadcrumbs
2 teaspoons Dijon mustard
2 teaspoons Worcestershire sauce
¼ cup fresh parsley leaves, chopped
4 hamburger buns
¼ teaspoon ground black pepper

DIRECTIONS

1. Heat 1 tablespoon of oil in a skillet until shimmering and then add in onion. Cook the onions stirring occasionally for about 5 minutes until softened. Add garlic and allow to cook for an additional 1 minute, and then remove the pan from heat.
2. Mash beans with a fork in a bowl. Add onion to the mashed beans, add breadcrumbs, parsley, lemon juice, flax egg, mustard, salt, Worcestershire sauce and pepper, and mix well until combined. Cover and refrigerate the bowl for 1-2 hours.
3. Divide the mixture into 4 portions. Shape each portion into ½-inch thick patty.
4. Heat 1 tablespoon of oil in a frying pan until shimmering (over medium heat), then add the patties. Cook for about 5-6 minutes until it turns golden brown, then flip and continue cooking for another 5-6 minutes on the other side.
5. Place the cooked burgers on top of buns and add your desired toppings, and then serve.

Quinoa Stuffed Peppers

PREPARATION TIME
15'

COOK TIME
1H 20'

SERVING
8

NUTRITION

Calories: 248
Fat: 4.3g
Total carbs: 43.7g
Protein: 9.6g

INGREDIENTS

2 garlic cloves, chopped
1 tablespoon and ½ teaspoon olive oil
1 (½) teaspoons ground cumin
1 onion, diced
A pinch and 1 teaspoon salt
1 cup quinoa, rinsed
8 bell peppers
4 tablespoons tomato paste
1 can (15 ounces) of black beans, drained and rinsed
1 (½) teaspoons chili powder
1 (½) cups corn kernels, fresh or frozen
2 cups water
Freshly ground black pepper to taste
½ cup fresh cilantro, chopped

DIRECTIONS

1. Preheat the oven to 375°F. Pour water into the baking dish just enough to cover the bottom of the baking dish and set aside.
2. Heat 1 tablespoon of oil in a saucepan over medium heat until shimmering, and then add the onion. Season with salt and cook for about 8 minutes stirring occasionally until the onions are softened.
3. Add quinoa to the saucepan with onions and cook for about 2 minutes as you stir occasionally.
4. Add tomato paste to the cooking saucepan along with garlic, chili powder and cumin. Cook for about 2 minutes as you stir occasionally until fragrant.
5. Add 2 cups of water and 1 teaspoon of salt to the saucepan and season with pepper. Stir well to combine.
6. Bring to a boil and reduce the heat to the lowest setting. Cover the saucepan with a tight-fitting lid and cook for 15 minutes undisturbed.
7. In the meantime, prepare the bell peppers. Remove tops from peppers, remove the core. Drizzle with about ½ teaspoon of oil and season generously with pepper and salt. Set the bell peppers aside.
8. Remove quinoa from heat when ready. Allow the quinoa to stand covered for 5 minutes, fluff it gently with a fork. Add beans, corn and cilantro to the pan with quinoa and stir well to combine. Taste and adjust on salt and pepper.
9. Divide the mixture evenly among the peppers and top with caps. Place stuffed peppers into the prepared baking dish in a single layer.
10. Cover tightly with aluminum foil and then bake for about 1 hour. Uncover and let rest for 5 minutes. Enjoy!

Tofu Chickpea Stir-Fry

PREPARATION TIME
5'

COOK TIME
20'

SERVING
4

NUTRITION

Calories: 438
Fat: 15.4g
Total carbs: 61g
Protein: 15.7g

INGREDIENTS

Toasted sesame seeds to taste
Minced chives to taste

FOR THE SAUCE:
2 tablespoons rice vinegar
1/3 cup water
2 teaspoons maple syrup
1/4 cup tahini
1 teaspoon fresh ginger, minced
2 tablespoons tamari or soy sauce

FOR THE STIR-FRY:
1/2 red onion, thinly sliced
1 tablespoon peanut oil
1 bell pepper, cored, seeded, diced
1 cup chickpeas, cooked or canned
8 ounces baked tofu, cubed
2 teaspoons fresh ginger, chopped

DIRECTIONS

1. Prepare the sauce by stirring together the sauce ingredients in a bowl.
2. Prepare the stir-fry. Heat oil in a skillet or wok over medium-high heat until shimmering, add in chickpeas as you stir, for about 2 minutes.
3. Stir the minced ginger into the skillet and cook for an additional 1 minute. Add onion and peppers to the skillet and cook for about 2-3 minutes until the onions are tender.
4. Toss the baked tofu into the skillet and cook for about 4-6 minutes as you stir until the tofu is golden and chickpeas are brown. Pour tahini sauce over the tofu and cook for 1 minute more until the sauce has heated through.
5. Serve and enjoy topped with toasted sesame seeds and minced chives.

Smoky Burrito Tempeh

PREPARATION TIME
5'

COOK TIME
30'

SERVING
4

NUTRITION

Calories: 602
Fat: 21.8g
Total carbs: 79g
Protein: 28.7g

INGREDIENTS

1/2 teaspoon cumin powder
1 (15 ounces) can of black beans
1 cup brown rice, cooked
A pinch of sea salt
1 lime
A handful of fresh cilantro
FOR THE TEMPEH:
1-inch water
10 ounces tempeh, cubed
1 tablespoon olive oil
FOR THE MARINADE:
2 garlic cloves, minced
1 tablespoon olive oil
1/2 white onion, diced
1 whole chipotle pepper in adobo sauce, canned, plus 1 tablespoon sauce
1 (15 ounces) can tomato sauce

DIRECTIONS

1. Steam the tempeh. Add 1-inch of water to a saucepan and then bring to a simmer. Insert a steamer basket, add the tempeh. Cover and steam for 15 minutes. Cube the tempeh once steamed and set aside.
2. Prepare the sauce. Heat a skillet over medium heat until hot and then add oil and onion. Cook as you stir frequently for about 3 minutes until soft and slightly browned.
3. Add garlic to the skillet and cook for 1-2 minutes more. Add tomato sauce to the skillet along with adobo sauce and chipotle pepper. Stir and heat until bubbly.
4. Turn down the heat to low and simmer for 3-4 minutes, and then transfer the sauce to a blender. Blend on high until the sauce is completely smooth.
5. Return the sauce to the skillet, then turn down the heat to low. Allow the sauce to cook as you stir occasionally until it has thickened.
6. Add black beans to a saucepan and heat over medium heat until bubbling. Reduce the heat and add in cumin and a pinch of sea salt. Stir and reduce the heat to low. Mash the beans with a wooden spoon (optional).
7. Heat a separate skillet over medium heat until hot. Add oil and the steamed tempeh, cook for about 6-8 minutes until crisp and brown on all sides. Add tempeh to the red sauce and stir gently to coat well.
8. Cover and let rest for about 2-3 minutes. Divide the beans, rice, vegetables of choice and tempeh between the serving bowls and garnish with lime and fresh cilantro. Enjoy!

Sweet and Sour Tempeh

PREPARATION TIME
5'

COOK TIME
25'

SERVING
2

NUTRITION

Calories: 491
Fat: 12g
Total carbs: 52g
Protein: 24g

INGREDIENTS

Brown rice to taste
Chunks of pineapple to taste
Sesame seeds to taste
FOR THE STIR-FRY:
1 tablespoon sunflower oil
1/2 bell pepper, cut into chunks or slices
1 packet gluten-free tempeh, cut into squares
A large handful of snow peas
1 brown onion, diced
1 teaspoon sesame oil
FOR THE SWEET AND SOUR SAUCE:
1 tablespoon ketchup
2 teaspoons cornstarch dissolved in 4 teaspoons of water
1/3 cup rice vinegar
1 teaspoon tamari
1/4 cup coconut sugar

DIRECTIONS

1. Add all the ingredients for the sauce to a saucepan and turn the heat on. Bring everything to a boil, then turn off the heat. Add cornstarch mixture slowly and gradually, stirring constantly until thickened. Set aside.
2. Preheat sesame and sunflower oil in a pan over medium-high heat. Fry tempeh until all sides are browned.
3. Add diced onion and fry until browned, for 2 to 3 minutes. Add in the prepped veggies and cook for a few minutes.
4. Pour in the prepared sweet and sour sauce and cook for 1 to 2 minutes.
5. Serve over brown rice and top with chunks of pineapple and sesame seeds, if desired.

Korean Braised Tofu

PREPARATION TIME
5'

COOK TIME
15'

SERVING
4

NUTRITION

Calories: 226
Fat: 12g
Total carbs: 11g
Protein: 19g

INGREDIENTS

½-1 tablespoon Korean chili powder
Toasted sesame seeds for garnish (optional)
1 onion, cut into thin slices
1 scallion, cut into thin slices
1 (14 ounces) block firm tofu, cut into 16 squares
4 tablespoons sake
1 tablespoon sugar
2 tablespoons soy sauce

DIRECTIONS

1. Add slices of onion into a frying pan/nonstick skillet and top with tofu slices.
2. Combine together 3 tablespoons soy sauce, 1 tablespoon sugar, 4 tablespoons sake and ½-1 tablespoon Korean chili powder. Pour over tofu and cover the pan.
3. Raise the heat and cook everything until boiling.
4. Now reduce the heat to medium and cook for 4 to 5 minutes.
5. Uncover the pan and raise the heat again. Cook until the sauce has been reduced.
6. Remove from heat and transfer the Korean braised tofu to a serving platter.
7. Garnish with sesame seeds and scallions and enjoy!

Red Lentil Tikka Masala

INGREDIENTS

PREPARATION TIME
5'

COOK TIME
30'

1 (1/2) tablespoon garam masala
2 tablespoons olive oil
1/4 cup cilantro, chopped
1 onion, diced
1/2 cup coconut milk
1 small Serrano or jalapeno pepper, minced
1 cup red lentils
1 tablespoon ginger, grated
1 (1/2) cups vegetable broth
3 garlic cloves, minced
1 tablespoon coconut sugar
1 tablespoon tomato paste
1 (28 ounces) can of crushed tomatoes

SERVING
4

NUTRITION

Calories: 708
Fat: 15g
Total carbs: 56g
Protein: 30g

DIRECTIONS

1. Preheat olive oil in a pan over medium heat and sauté Serrano pepper and onion for few minutes until softened.
2. Add in 1 tablespoon tomato paste, 1 1/2 tablespoons garam masala, 1 tablespoon ginger and 3 minced cloves of garlic. Stir for a minute, until fragrant.
3. Now add in 1 1/2 cups vegetable broth, 1 tablespoon coconut sugar and a can of crushed tomatoes. Stir well until combined, then add 1 cup red lentils.
4. Turn the heat down and simmer covered for 25 to 30 minutes until lentils are tender.
5. Stir in 1/4 cup chopped cilantro and 1/2 cup coconut milk. Serve and enjoy!

Thai Red Tofu Curry

PREPARATION TIME
5'

COOK TIME
30'

SERVING
4

NUTRITION

Calories: 602
Fat: 21.8g
Total carbs: 79g
Protein: 28.7g

INGREDIENTS

Rice to taste

FOR THE TOFU AND MARINADE:
2 tablespoons sesame oil
3 tablespoons cornstarch
16 ounces extra-firm tofu, drained, pressed and cut into cubes
1 teaspoon red pepper flakes
1 garlic clove, minced
2 tablespoons rice vinegar
3 tablespoons soy sauce or tamari
1 tablespoon brown sugar
1 tablespoon coconut oil

FOR THE CURRY:
3 tablespoons red curry paste
1 small yellow onion, minced
8 fresh Thai basil leaves cut into strips
2 large cloves garlic, minced
1 lime juice and zest
1 teaspoon of ginger, grated
1 red bell pepper, sliced
1 tablespoon soy sauce or tamari
1 cup Cremini mushrooms, sliced
13 ounces light coconut milk
¼ cup water

DIRECTIONS

1. Add 3 tablespoons soy sauce or tamari, 2 tablespoons sesame oil, 1 tablespoon brown sugar, 1 teaspoon red pepper flakes, garlic and 2 tablespoons rice vinegar to a bowl. Mix well.
2. Add tofu cubes to a freezer bag and pour in the marinade. Shake well until coated and marinate for at least half an hour or up to 1 day. Transfer to a bowl and add in 3 tablespoons of cornstarch. Toss well.
3. Preheat coconut oil in a pan over medium-high heat and fry each side of tofu cubes for approximately 2 minutes until crispy and golden brown. Once done, transfer to a bowl.
4. Simmer ¼ cup of water in a saucepan. Add garlic, 1 teaspoon of grated ginger and minced onion.
5. Simmer until onions are translucent, for about 5 minutes over medium heat.
6. Add mushrooms, red bell pepper slices and 3 tablespoons of red curry paste. Stir well until all veggies are coated.
7. Now add 1 tablespoon soy sauce or tamari, 13 ounces light coconut milk, lime zest and juice.
8. Stir well and let the curry simmer for about 15 minutes.
9. Meanwhile, prepare rice as per directions mentioned on the package. Once done, transfer to a serving bowl and spoon curry on top, followed by crispy tofu and Thai basil strips.

Barbecue Baked Seitan Strips

PREPARATION TIME
10'

COOK TIME
60'

SERVING
8

NUTRITION

Calories: 286
Fat: 22g
Total carbs: 14g
Protein: 19g

INGREDIENTS

FOR THE DOUGH:
1/2 teaspoon dried oregano
2 tablespoons soy sauce
2 cups vital wheat gluten
2 tablespoons olive oil
1/2 cup nutritional yeast
2 tablespoons maple syrup
1 (1/2) tablespoons garlic powder
1 (1/2) cups vegetable broth
1 teaspoon smoked paprika
1 cup vegan barbecue sauce, store-bought or homemade
1 teaspoon onion powder
1/2 teaspoon dried basil
1/2 teaspoon ground black pepper

FOR THE MARINADE:
2 tablespoons soy sauce
1/2 teaspoons paprika
2 cups vegetable broth
1 teaspoon garlic powder
1 cup vegan barbecue sauce, store-bought or homemade
1 teaspoon ground black pepper
2 tablespoons maple syrup
1 teaspoon liquid smoke
2 tablespoons olive oil
2 teaspoons hot sauce (optional)

DIRECTIONS

1. To a bowl, add 1/2 teaspoon dried basil, 2 cups vital wheat gluten, 1/2 teaspoon dried oregano, 1/2 cup nutritional yeast, 1 teaspoon smoked paprika, 1/2 teaspoon ground black pepper, 1 (1/2) tablespoons garlic powder and 1 teaspoon onion powder. Mix well.
2. Take another bowl and combine together 1 (1/2) cups vegetable broth, 1 cup vegan barbecue sauce, 2 tablespoons maple syrup, 2 tablespoons soy sauce and 2 tablespoons olive oil. Pour this mixture over the dry ingredients and mix with your hands. Knead for a few minutes. Add more broth if needed.
3. Add all the marinade ingredients to a bowl and mix well until combined. Place the dough onto a flat surface and slightly flatten it with your hands.
4. Spread a bit of olive oil on top of the dough to prevent sticking. Then roll out the dough into a 9 x 12-inch rectangular shape ½-1-inch thick.
5. Add a cup of marinade to a roasting dish and lay rolled-out the dough on top. Pour the remaining marinade over the dough and bake in a preheated oven at 390°F, for about 1 hour.
6. After half an hour, add one more cup of broth if it's too dry. Once done, serve right away and enjoy!

Teriyaki Glazed Tofu Steaks

PREPARATION TIME
5'

COOK TIME
15'

SERVING
3

NUTRITION

Calories: 239
Fat: 15.4g
Total carbs: 4g
Protein: 21g

INGREDIENTS

FOR THE TERIYAKI SAUCE:
2 tablespoons maple syrup
1/4 teaspoon cornstarch
1/2 teaspoon ginger, grated
1/4 teaspoon Dijon mustard
1 teaspoon minced garlic
1 tablespoon apple cider vinegar or rice vinegar
1 tablespoon lemon juice
4 tablespoons soy sauce

FOR THE TOFU STEAKS:
Oil for coating the pan
1 (14 ounces) block extra-firm tofu, cut into 1/2-inch thick slices

DIRECTIONS

1. Add all the teriyaki sauce ingredients to a bowl and mix well. Coat a skillet-pan with oil and warm it up.
2. Add tofu steaks to the pan in batches and cook until both sides are covered with a golden-brown crust.
3. Pour in half of the prepared sauce when one batch is done and cook for about 2 minutes until the sauce thickens.
4. Similarly cook the remaining tofu. Serve immediately!

Chili Sin Carne

PREPARATION TIME
5'

COOK TIME
30'

SERVING
6

NUTRITION

Calories: 340
Fat: 18g
Total carbs: 42g
Protein: 25g

INGREDIENTS

1 teaspoon ground cumin
1 cup vegetable stock
2 tablespoons olive oil
1 pound frozen soy mince
2 garlic cloves, minced
½ ounce split red lentils
1 red onion, thinly sliced
1 tin (14 ounces) red kidney beans, drained and rinsed
2 celery stalks, chopped
28 ounces tinned chopped tomatoes
2 carrots, peeled and chopped
2 red peppers, chopped
1 teaspoon chili powder
Salt and pepper to taste

DIRECTIONS

1. Add oil to a pan and preheat over medium-high heat.
2. Sauté peppers, celery, garlic, carrots and onion until softened for a few minutes.
3. Stir in pepper, salt and 1 teaspoon of each chili powder and cumin.
4. Add in red lentils, vegetable stock, chopped tomatoes, red kidney beans and frozen soy mince. Simmer everything for approximately 25 minutes.
5. If you want, serve with steamed basmati rice and some freshly torn coriander (optional). Finish with a drizzle of lime juice. Enjoy!

Teriyaki Tofu Stir-Fry

PREPARATION TIME
5'

COOK TIME
20'

SERVING
4

NUTRITION

Calories: 411
Fat: 11g
Total carbs: 58g
Protein: 19g

INGREDIENTS

1 tablespoon tamari or soy sauce
2 teaspoons cooking oil
14 ounces firm tofu, cut the block into half, pressed
2 teaspoons red chili sauce (optional)
1 pound asparagus, trimmed and chopped
2 tablespoons green onions, chopped

FOR THE SAUCE:
5 garlic cloves, minced
1/2 cup water
3 tablespoons tamari or soy sauce
2 teaspoons cornstarch
1 tablespoon sesame oil
1/4 cup coconut sugar or maple syrup
1 tablespoon rice vinegar
1/2 tablespoon ginger, grated

FOR SERVING:
4 cups quinoa, cooked or brown rice

DIRECTIONS

1. Cut tofu into 1/2-inch cubes. Add a teaspoon of oil to a pan and fry tofu cubes over medium heat. Cook until tofu is lightly brown on most sides, flipping frequently.
2. Add a bit of oil if tofu is sticking to the pan.
3. Once done, toss tofu cubes with a tablespoon of soy sauce or tamari.
4. Transfer to a bowl and set aside. Wipe the pan quickly with a wet paper napkin.
5. Combine together all the ingredients for the sauce in a bowl and set aside.
6. Sauté asparagus in a wiped pan along with a teaspoon of oil until crispy. Transfer to fried tofu.
7. Now, add in the sauce and cook until the sauce begins to thicken.
8. Add more coconut sugar or tamari, if desired.
9. Stir in green onions and red chili paste. Turn off the heat, serve and enjoy! (Over cooked quinoa or rice).

Farro Protein Bowl

PREPARATION TIME
5'

COOK TIME
30'

SERVING
4

NUTRITION

Calories: 590
Fat: 17.8g
Total carbs: 92g
Protein: 18g

INGREDIENTS

1 (1/4) cups water
4 lemon wedges
1 cup sweet potatoes, diced
2 tablespoons roasted almonds
1 cup carrots, diced
1/4 cup hummus
2 teaspoons oil
2 cups mixed greens
1 (15 ounces) can chickpeas, drained and rinsed
Salt and pepper to taste
4 ounces smoky tempeh strips
1/2 cup farro, uncooked

DIRECTIONS

1. Toss carrots and potatoes with a pinch of pepper, salt and 1 teaspoon of oil. Spread out on a third of the baking sheet in a single layer.
2. Now toss chickpeas with 2 pinches of pepper, salt and 1 teaspoon of oil, until coated. Spread out on second and third of the baking sheet, in a single layer.
3. Place strips of tempeh on the remaining third of the sheet. Roast in a preheated oven at 375°F, for half an hour.
4. Flip over the strips of tempeh and stir chickpeas and potatoes (while keeping them separate).
5. Meanwhile, add 1 (1/4) cups water to a pot along with a hefty pinch of salt and farro grains. Cover and bring everything to a boil. Then turn the heat down and cook until grains are chewy, for about 25 to 30 minutes.
6. Once done, divide greens and farro among 2 bowls.
7. When tempeh, chickpeas and potatoes are done, sprinkle with salt if needed and divide among the bowls. Top with lemon wedges, almonds and hummus. Serve and enjoy!

Mongolian Seitan

PREPARATION TIME
5'

COOK TIME
20'

SERVING
6

NUTRITION

Calories: 324
Fat: 8g
Total carbs: 33g
Protein: 29g

INGREDIENTS

FOR THE SAUCE:
1/3 teaspoon red pepper flakes
2 tablespoons cold water
2 teaspoons vegetable oil
2 teaspoons cornstarch
1/2 teaspoon ginger, minced or grated
1/2 cup + 2 tablespoons coconut sugar
3 cloves garlic, minced or grated
1/2 cup low-sodium soy sauce
1/3 teaspoon Chinese five-spice (optional)

FOR THE SEITAN:
1 pound homemade or store-bought seitan, cut into 1-inch pieces
1 1/2 tablespoons vegetable oil

DIRECTIONS

1. Preheat oil in a pan and sauté garlic and ginger for 30 seconds, stirring constantly. Then add 1/3 teaspoon Chinese five-spice (if using) and 1/3 teaspoon red pepper flakes. Cook until fragrant, for about 40 to 60 seconds.
2. Stir in 1/2 cup low-sodium soy sauce and 1/2 cup + 2 tablespoons coconut sugar. Turn the heat down and simmer for 5 to 7 minutes, until sugar is completely dissolved, stirring occasionally.
3. Whisk cornstarch in cold water and stir in a pan slowly and gradually. Cook until the sauce has thickened for a few minutes. Turn the heat down and simmer until ready to add to seitan.
4. Preheat oil in a skillet over medium-high heat. Cook seitan until crisped and lightly browned, for 4 to 5 minutes.
5. Turn down the heat and add in the sauce. Stir well until all seitan pieces are coated with sauce.
6. Serve along with your favorite veggies and/or rice and garnish with scallions and toasted sesame seeds, if you want (optional).

Black Bean and Quinoa Balls

PREPARATION TIME
5'

COOK TIME
60'

SERVING
4

NUTRITION

Calories: 241
Fat: 15g
Total carbs: 16g
Protein: 15g

INGREDIENTS

4 zucchinis, spiralized
Salt and pepper to taste
2 tablespoons tomato paste
½ cup quinoa
1 tablespoon chopped fresh herbs (oregano, rosemary, sage, basil)
1 can of black beans
1 teaspoon garlic powder
¼ cup sesame seeds
2 tablespoons nutritional yeast
¼ cup of oat flour or breadcrumbs
½ tablespoon Sriracha
1 cup water

FOR THE SAUCE:
2 tablespoons toasted pine nuts
Salt and pepper to taste
½ cup cherry tomatoes, halved
1 teaspoon oregano
½ cup sun-dried tomatoes
A handful of fresh basil
1 tablespoon apple cider vinegar
2 tablespoons nutritional yeast
1 garlic clove
Fresh basil to serve

DIRECTIONS

1. Add quinoa to a pot along with a cup of water and cook for 15 minutes. Once done, drain well and allow it to cool a bit.
2. In the meantime, mash coarsely black beans in a bowl by using a fork or masher. Add in oat flour (or breadcrumbs), tomato paste, cooked quinoa, sesame seeds, nutritional yeast, Sriracha and spices. Mix with your hands until the dough is formed.
3. Now make 22 to 25 balls from the dough. Place balls onto a parchment-lined baking sheet.
4. Bake for about 35 to 40 minutes at 400°F, until crispy.
5. Meanwhile, blend all the sauce ingredients (except cherry tomatoes and sun-dried tomatoes) in a blender, until creamy.
6. Add zucchinis to a bowl along with cherry tomatoes and sun-dried tomatoes. Mix well.
7. Top with baked black bean and quinoa balls (3-4 balls per serving). Garnish with fresh basil, fresh herbs and serve right away!

Teriyaki Tempeh Tacos

PREPARATION TIME
5'

COOK TIME
20'

SERVING
6

NUTRITION

Calories: 216
Fat: 13g
Total carbs: 15g
Protein: 10g

INGREDIENTS

6 gluten-free taco shells
8 ounces package of organic tempeh
1 tablespoon of coconut oil
1/4 teaspoon onion powder
3 tablespoons veggie broth
1/2 teaspoon garlic powder
1 tablespoon tamari or soy sauce

FOR THE ASIAN SLAW:
1 cup red cabbage, shredded
3 scallions, chopped
1 cup green cabbage, shredded
1 cup carrots, grated

FOR THE DRESSING:
2 tablespoons maple syrup
1/4 teaspoon pepper
1 teaspoon rice wine/apple cider vinegar
1/4 teaspoon salt
1 tablespoon sesame oil or Extra virgin olive oil
1 teaspoon Sriracha
1 tablespoon lime juice
1 tablespoon Dijon mustard
1/4 cup tamari or soy sauce
1/4 teaspoon liquid smoke
1/2 teaspoon cornstarch
1/2 teaspoon garlic powder

DIRECTIONS

1. Take an 8 ounces package of organic tempeh and cut it into squares or triangles. Transfer to a steamer basket and steam for about 10 minutes.
2. Meanwhile, prepare the marinade by whisking together the onion powder, veggie broth, garlic powder and tamari (or soy sauce).
3. Once the tempeh is cooked, transfer to a dish and pour the marinade on top. Let it sit for about 20 minutes.
4. Preheat a tablespoon of coconut oil in a pan and sear each side of tempeh for 3 to 5 minutes until crispy.
5. Meanwhile, prepare teriyaki sauce. For this, take a bowl and mix together the liquid smoke, tamari (or soy sauce), cornstarch, sesame (or olive) oil, garlic powder, Sriracha, maple syrup and rice wine/apple cider vinegar.
6. When the tempeh is cooked, add to teriyaki sauce and toss well until the tempeh is coated completely.
7. Now take out the tempeh from the sauce and add it back to the pan. Heat each side for 30 seconds, then turn off the heat.
8. Top with the remaining sauce and let it sit for a minute.
9. Add all the dressing ingredients to a bowl and mix well. Take another bowl and mix together all the slaw ingredients.
10. Combine both dressing and the slaw ingredients together. Top tacos with slaw-dressing mixture and tempeh.

Spinach Ricotta Lasagna

PREPARATION TIME
5'

COOK TIME
40'

SERVING
4

NUTRITION

Calories: 473
Fat: 8g
Total carbs: 85g
Protein: 14g

INGREDIENTS

VEGAN RICOTTA FILLING:
½ teaspoon salt
1 pound firm tofu, broken into big chunks
5 garlic cloves
1 tablespoon mustard
2 tablespoons olive oil
A pinch of black pepper
2 lemons, juiced
A pinch of nutmeg

FOR THE CREAM SAUCE:
3 tablespoons flour
½ teaspoon salt
3 tablespoons margarine
3 cups soy milk

FOR THE TOMATO SAUCE:
Generous pinch salt
½ pound lasagna sheets
1 cup passata
1 pound frozen spinach, defrosted, drained
2 teaspoons dried oregano
A pinch of black pepper

DIRECTIONS

1. To a blender, add all the filling ingredients except for tofu and blend well until creamy and smooth. Now add in tofu chunks and blend until you obtain a crumbly filling.
2. Add margarine to a pan and allow it to melt over medium heat. Then stir in flour until you obtained a thick paste. Whisk in salt and milk until thickened.
3. Add passata to a bowl along with salt, pepper and oregano. Mix well.
4. Spread tomato sauce on the bottom of the baking dish. Add lasagna sheets on top.
5. Add filling and cream sauce. Repeat layers until all the ingredients are used.
6. Cover the last layer of lasagna sheet with creamy and tomato sauce. Cook at 375°F for about 30-40 minutes.
7. Once done, serve immediately and enjoy!

Samosa Pie

PREPARATION TIME
10'

COOK TIME
20'

SERVING
4

NUTRITION

Calories: 936
Fat: 47.9g
Total carbs: 50.4g
Protein: 91.1g

INGREDIENTS

2 cans lentils, drained and rinsed
2 tablespoons vegetable oil
2 potatoes, peeled and diced
1 pack filo pastry, defrosted (if frozen)
5 ounces frozen green peas
1 tablespoon vegetable oil
1 teaspoon chili powder
1 onion, diced
1 tablespoon dried coriander
3 garlic cloves, minced
2 tablespoons curry powder
Salt and pepper to taste

DIRECTIONS

1. Boil water in a large pot and add potatoes. Cook until soft, then add in frozen green peas in the last minute of cooking. Drain well and mash both peas and potatoes together.
2. In the meantime, preheat oil in a pan over medium heat and sauté garlic and onion until softened.
3. Add in the curry powder, chili powder and dried coriander, and continue cooking for a minute further. Then add lentils along with a drop of water and cook over low heat for about 10 minutes.
4. Now add mashed potatoes and peas to a pan with soy mince and sprinkle with pepper and salt. If it's too dry, add a bit of water.
5. Transfer mixture to an oven dish and spread evenly. Now unfold filo pastry and start layering on top of potato mixture, sheet by sheet.
6. Brush each layer with some oil. Cook in a preheated oven at 350°F, for about 20 minutes, until crispy and golden.
7. Serve and enjoy!

Lentil Roast with Balsamic Onion Gravy

PREPARATION TIME
5'

COOK TIME
45'

SERVING
6

NUTRITION

Calories: 387
Fat: 28.7g
Total carbs: 25g
Protein: 13g

INGREDIENTS

FOR THE LENTIL LOAF:
1 can (14 ounces) cooked kidney beans, rinsed
5 ounces rolled oats
1 tablespoon vegetable oil
Black pepper to taste
1 onion, minced
4 tablespoons nutritional yeast
3 garlic cloves, minced
2 tablespoons mixed dried herbs
2 portobello mushrooms, chopped
1 tablespoon gluten-free tamari soy sauce
1 carrot, grated
1 can (14 ounces) cooked puy lentils, rinsed

FOR THE BALSAMIC ONION GRAVY:
1 tablespoon coconut sugar or brown sugar
3 tablespoons gluten-free tamari soy sauce
2 cups vegetable stock
3 tablespoons balsamic vinegar
1 red onion, sliced
1 cup red wine
2 tablespoons vegetable oil
1 tablespoon arrowroot powder

DIRECTIONS

1. Sauté garlic and onion in oil until soft. Then add in carrots and mushrooms and continue cooking for further 5 minutes.
2. Add the remaining ingredients and mash to combine. If the mixture is too wet, add some oats, if it's too dry, then add a bit of water.
3. Transfer mixture to a greaseproof paper-lined loaf tin and cook in a preheated oven at 350°F, for about 40 to 45 minutes.
4. Sauté onion in oil along with sugar for about 10 minutes. Then stir in arrowroot powder and cook for a few minutes.
5. Add in vegetable stock, tamari sauce, vinegar and wine, and simmer at low until stock is reduced by half.
6. Cook until you have thick and dark gravy. Serve warm with roast vegetables and lentil loaf.

Chapter 7
Salads Recipes

Arugula with Fruits and Nuts

PREPARATION TIME
10'

COOK TIME
0'

SERVING
1

NUTRITION

Calories: 160
Fat: 7g
Carbohydrate: 25g
Protein: 3g

INGREDIENTS

½ cup arugula
½ peach
½ red onion
¼ cup blueberries
5 walnuts, chopped
1 tablespoon extra-virgin olive oil
2 tablespoons red wine vinegar
1 spring of fresh basil

DIRECTIONS

1. Halve the peach and remove the seed. Heat a grill pan and grill it briefly on both sides. Cut the red onion into thin half-rings. Roughly chop the pecans.
2. Heat a pan and roast the pecans in it until they are fragrant.
3. Place the arugula on a plate and spread peaches, red onions, blueberries and roasted pecans over it.
4. Put all the ingredients for the dressing in a food processor and mix to an even dressing. Drizzle the dressing over the salad.

Broccoli Salad

PREPARATION TIME
25'

COOK TIME
0'

SERVING
2

NUTRITION

Calories: 230
Fat: 18g
Carbohydrate: 35g
Protein: 10g

INGREDIENTS

1 head of broccoli
1/2 red onion
2 carrots, grated
1/4 cup red grapes
2 1/2 tablespoons coconut yogurt
1 tablespoon water
1 teaspoon mustard
1 pinch salt

DIRECTIONS

1. Cut the broccoli into florets and cook for 8 minutes. Cut the red onion into thin half-rings. Halve the grapes. Mix coconut yogurt, water and mustard with a pinch of salt to make the dressing.
2. Drain the broccoli and rinse with ice-cold water to stop the cooking process.
3. Mix the broccoli with the carrot, onion and red grapes in a bowl. Serve the dressing separately on the side.

Brunoise Salad

PREPARATION TIME
10'

COOK TIME
0'

SERVING
2

NUTRITION

Calories: 84
Carbohydrate: 3g
Fat: 4g
Protein: 0g

INGREDIENTS

1 tomato
1 zucchini
½ red bell pepper
½ yellow bell pepper
½ red onion
3 springs fresh parsley
½ lemon
2 tablespoons olive oil
Salt and pepper to taste

DIRECTIONS

1. Finely dice tomato, peppers, zucchini and red onion to get a brunoise. Mix all the cubes in a bowl. Chop parsley and mix in the salad. Squeeze the lemon over the salad and add the olive oil.
2. Season with salt and pepper.

Brussels Sprouts and Ricotta Salad

PREPARATION TIME
15'

COOK TIME
0'

SERVING
2

NUTRITION

Calories: 353
Fat: 4.8g
Carbohydrate: 28.1g
Protein: 28.3g

INGREDIENTS

1 (½) cups Brussels sprouts, thinly sliced
1 green apple cut "à la julienne"
½ red onion
8 walnuts, chopped
1 teaspoon extra-virgin olive oil
1 tablespoon lemon juice
1 tablespoon orange juice
4 ounces ricotta cheese

DIRECTIONS

1. Put the red onion in a cup and cover it with boiling water. Let it rest 10 minutes, then drain and pat with a kitchen paper. Slice Brussels sprouts as thin as you can, cut the apple à la julienne (sticks).
2. Mix Brussels sprouts, onion and apple, and season them with oil, salt, pepper, lemon juice and orange juice, and spread it on a serving plate.
3. Spread a small spoonful of ricotta cheese over Brussels sprouts mixture and top with chopped walnuts.

Celery and Raisins Snack Salad

PREPARATION TIME
10'

COOK TIME
0'

SERVING
4

NUTRITION

Calories: 120
Fat: 1g
Carbohydrate: 6g
Protein: 5g

INGREDIENTS

½ cup raisins
4 cups celery, sliced
¼ cup parsley, chopped
½ cup walnuts, chopped
Juice of ½ lemon
2 tablespoons olive oil
Salt and black pepper to taste

DIRECTIONS

1. In a salad bowl, mix celery with raisins, walnuts, parsley, lemon juice, oil, salt and black pepper, toss.
2. Divide into small cups and serve as a snack.

Dijon Celery Salad

PREPARATION TIME
10'

COOK TIME
0'

SERVING
4

NUTRITION

Calories: 125
Fat: 2g
Carbohydrate: 7g
Protein 7g

INGREDIENTS

1/2 cup lemon juice
1/3 cup Dijon mustard
2/3 cup olive oil
Black pepper to taste
2 apples, cored, peeled and cubed
1 bunch celery roughly chopped
3/4 cup walnuts, chopped

DIRECTIONS

1. In a salad bowl, mix celery and its leaves with apple pieces and walnuts.
2. Add black pepper, lemon juice, mustard and olive oil, whisk well, add to your salad, toss, divide into small cups and serve.

Fresh Endive Salad

PREPARATION TIME
10'

COOK TIME
0'

SERVING
1

NUTRITION

Calories: 112
Fat: 11g
Carbohydrate: 2g
Protein: 0g

INGREDIENTS

1/2 red endive
1 orange
1 tomato
1/2 cucumber
1/2 red onion
Olive oil and fresh lemon juice to taste

DIRECTIONS

1. Cut off the hard stem of the endive and remove the leaves. Peel the orange and cut the pulp into wedges.
2. Cut the tomato and cucumber into small pieces. Cut the red onion into thin half-rings.
3. Place the endive boats on a plate; spread the orange wedges, tomato, cucumber and red onion over the boats. Drizzle some olive oil and fresh lemon juice and serve.

Fresh Salad with Orange Dressing

PREPARATION TIME
10'

COOK TIME
0'

SERVING
2

NUTRITION

Calories: 150
Fat: 10g
Carbohydrate: 11g
Protein: 2g

INGREDIENTS

½ cup lettuce
1 yellow bell pepper
1 red pepper
4 ounces carrot, grated
10 almonds
4 tablespoons extra-virgin olive oil
½ cup orange juice
1 tablespoon apple cider vinegar

DIRECTIONS

1. Clean the peppers and cut them into long, thin strips. Tear off the lettuce leaves and cut them into smaller pieces.
2. Mix the salad with the peppers and the carrots in a bowl. Roughly chop the almonds and sprinkle them over the salad.
3. Mix all the ingredients for the dressing in a bowl. Pour over the salad just before serving.

Greek Salad Skewers

PREPARATION TIME
10'

COOK TIME
0'

SERVING
2

NUTRITION

Calories: 236
Fat: 21g
Carbohydrate: 14g
Protein: 7g

INGREDIENTS

8 big black olives
8 cherry tomatoes
1 yellow pepper, cut into 8 squares
1/2 red onion, split into 8 wedges
1 cucumber, cut into 8 pieces
4 ounces feta, cut into 8 cubes
1 tablespoon extra-virgin olive oil
Juice of 1/2 lemon
1 teaspoon balsamic vinegar
1/2 teaspoon garlic, crushed

DIRECTIONS

1. Put the salad ingredients on the skewers following this order: cherry tomato, yellow pepper, red onion, cucumber, feta, black olive.
2. Repeat for each skewer and put on a serving plate.
3. As a dressing, put in a bowl: olive oil, a pinch of salt and pepper, lemon juice, balsamic vinegar and crushed garlic. Whisk well and drizzle on the skewers.

Moroccan Leeks Snack Salad

PREPARATION TIME
10'

COOK TIME
0'

SERVING
4

NUTRITION

Calories: 135
Fat: 1g
Carbohydrate: 18g
Protein: 9g

INGREDIENTS

1 bunch radishes, sliced
3 cups leeks, chopped
1 (½) cups olives, pitted and sliced
A pinch of turmeric powder
1 cup parsley, chopped
2 tablespoons extra-virgin olive oil
Black pepper to taste

DIRECTIONS

1. In a bowl, mix radishes with leeks, olives and parsley.
2. Add black pepper, oil and turmeric, toss to coat and serve.

Beans Snack Salad

PREPARATION TIME
10'

COOK TIME
0'

SERVING
6

NUTRITION

Calories: 120
Fat: 3g
Carbohydrate: 10g
Protein: 6g

INGREDIENTS

2 cups tomatoes, chopped
2 cups cucumber, chopped
2 cups beans, sprouted
2 cups clover sprouts
1 tablespoon cumin, ground
1 cup dill, chopped
4 tablespoons lemon juice
1 avocado, pitted and roughly chopped
1 cucumber, roughly chopped

DIRECTIONS

1. In a salad bowl, mix tomatoes with 2 cups cucumber, clover and sprouts.
2. In your blender, mix cumin with dill, lemon juice, 1 cucumber and 1 avocado, blend well, add this to your salad, toss well and serve.

Rainbow Salad

PREPARATION TIME
10'

COOK TIME
0'

SERVING
1

NUTRITION

Calories: 40
Fat: 1g
Carbohydrate: 5g
Protein: 2g

INGREDIENTS

1 cup lettuce
1/2 piece avocado
1 egg
1/4 green pepper and a pinch of salt
1/4 red bell pepper
2 tomatoes
1/2 red onion
1/2 carrot, grated
2 tablespoons olive oil
2 tablespoons red wine vinegar

DIRECTIONS

1. Boil the egg until done (6 minutes for soft boiled, 8 minutes for hard-boiled). Cool it under running water, peel it and cut it into slices.
2. Remove the seeds from the peppers and cut them into thin strips. Cut the tomatoes into small cubes. Cut the red onion into thin half-rings.
3. Cut the avocado into thin slices.
4. Place the salad on a plate and distribute all the vegetables in colorful rows.
5. Drizzle the vegetables with olive oil and red wine vinegar. Season with salt and pepper.

Roasted Butternut and Chickpeas Salad

PREPARATION TIME
10'

COOK TIME
30'

SERVING
4

NUTRITION

Calories: 353
Fat: 4.8g
Carbohydrate: 28.1g
Protein: 28.3g

INGREDIENTS

1 cup chickpeas, drained
1 pound butternut squash
2 cups kale
2 tablespoons olive oil
½ lemon, juiced
2 cloves of garlic
2 green apples
½ teaspoon honey
A pinch of salt and pepper

DIRECTIONS

1. Heat the oven to 400°F.
2. Cut the squash into medium cubes, put them in a baking tray, add drained chickpeas, garlic, 1 tablespoon oil, salt and pepper and mix. Cook for 25 minutes.
3. Mix the kale with the dressing: salt, pepper, lemon, olive oil and honey so that while the squash is cooking, it becomes softer and more pleasant to eat.
4. When squash and chickpeas are done, put them aside for 10 minutes, and in the meantime, chop the apples and mix them with kale.
5. Add squash and chickpeas on top and serve warm.

Salad with Cranberries and Apple

PREPARATION TIME
50'

COOK TIME
0'

SERVING
2

NUTRITION

Calories: 70
Fat: 3g
Carbohydrate: 6g
Protein: 7g

INGREDIENTS

1/2 cup arugula
1/2 apple
2 tablespoons cranberries
1/2 red onion
1/2 red bell pepper
10 walnuts
1 teaspoon mustard yellow
1 teaspoon honey
3 tablespoons extra-virgin olive oil
2 slices of bacon, chopped
1 teaspoon lemon juice
A pinch of salt and pepper

DIRECTIONS

1. Cut half the red onion into thin rings. Cut the bell pepper into small cubes. Cut the apple into four pieces and remove the core. Then cut into thin wedges. Drizzle some lemon juice on the apple wedges so that they do not change color.
2. Roughly chop walnuts. Mix the ingredients for the dressing in a bowl. Season with salt and pepper. Spread the lettuce on a plate and season with red pepper, red onions, apple wedges and walnuts.
3. Sprinkle bacon and cranberries over the salad. Drizzle the dressing over the salad and serve.

Sirt Fruit Salad

INGREDIENTS

1/2 cup matcha green tea
1 teaspoon honey
1 orange, halved
1 apple, cored and roughly chopped
10 red seedless grapes
10 blueberries

PREPARATION TIME
10'

COOK TIME
0'

SERVING
1

DIRECTIONS

1. Stir the honey into half a cup of green tea and let it chill.
2. When chilled, add the juice of half an orange.
3. Slice the other half and put in a bowl with the chopped apple, blueberries and grapes.
4. Cover with tea and let rest in the fridge for 30 minutes before serving.

NUTRITION

Calories: 110
Fat: 0g
Carbohydrate: 17g
Protein: 2g.

Sprouts and Apples Snack Salad

PREPARATION TIME
10'

COOK TIME
0'

SERVING
4

NUTRITION

Calories: 120
Fat: 2g
Carbohydrate: 8g
Protein: 6g

INGREDIENTS

1 pound Brussels sprouts, shredded
1 cup walnuts, chopped
1 apple, cored and cubed
1 red onion, chopped
3 tablespoons red vinegar
1 tablespoon mustard
½ cup olive oil
1 garlic clove, crushed
Black pepper to taste

DIRECTIONS

1. In a salad bowl, mix sprouts with apple, onion and walnuts.
2. In another bowl, mix vinegar with mustard, oil, garlic and pepper, whisk well, add this to your salad, toss well and serve as a snack.

Tomato and Avocado Salad

INGREDIENTS

1 tomato
4 ounces cherry tomatoes
1/2 red onion
1 ripe avocado
1 teaspoon fresh oregano
1 tablespoon extra-virgin olive oil
1 teaspoon red wine vinegar
1 pinch Celtic sea salt

PREPARATION TIME
10'

COOK TIME
0'

SERVING
1

DIRECTIONS

1. Cut the tomato into thick slices. Cut half of the cherry tomatoes into slices and the remaining in half. Cut the red onion into super-thin half rings (if you have it, use a mandolin slicer for this).
2. Cut the avocado into 6 parts. Spread the tomatoes on a plate, place the avocado on top.
3. Sprinkle red onion and oregano and drizzle olive oil, vinegar and a pinch of salt on the salad.

NUTRITION

Calories: 165
Fat: 14g
Carbohydrate: 7g
Protein: 5g

Avocado-Potato Salad

PREPARATION TIME
10'

COOK TIME
0'

SERVING
2

NUTRITION

Calories: 213
Fat: 9g
Carbohydrate: 28g
Protein: 3g

INGREDIENTS

1 ripe avocado, mashed
6 Yukon gold or red potatoes
1/2 cup red onion, chopped
2 ribs of celery, chopped
1/2 cup sweet red bell pepper
1 handful parsley, chopped

DIRECTIONS

1. Steam and cook the potatoes until tender, but not too soft. Stir thoroughly with all other ingredients.
2. Keep refrigerated until ready to serve.

Avocado with Raspberry Vinegar Salad

PREPARATION TIME
25'

COOK TIME
0'

SERVING
2

NUTRITION

Calories: 163
Fat: 4g
Carbohydrate: 15g
Protein: 14g

INGREDIENTS

4 ounces raspberries
3 ounces red wine vinegar
1 teaspoon extra-virgin olive oil
2 firm-ripe avocados
¼ cup radicchio

DIRECTIONS

1. Place half the raspberries in a bowl. Heat the vinegar in a saucepan until it starts to bubble and then pour it over the raspberries, then leave to steep for 5 minutes.
2. Strain the raspberries, pressing the fruit gently to extract all the juices but not the pulp.
3. Whisk the strained raspberry vinegar together with the oils and seasonings and then set aside.
4. Carefully halve each avocado and twist out the stone.
5. Peel away the skin and cut the flesh straight into the dressing.
6. Stir gently until the avocados are entirely covered in the dressing.
7. Cover tightly and then chill in the fridge for 2 hours.
8. Meanwhile, separate the radicchio leaves, rinse and drain them, and then dry them on kitchen paper. Store in the fridge in a polythene bag.
9. To serve, place a few radicchio leaves on individual plates.
10. Spoon on the avocado, stir and trim with the remaining raspberries.

Bitter Greens, Sprouts, Avocado and Orange Salad

PREPARATION TIME
5'

COOK TIME
0'

SERVING
4

NUTRITION

Calories: 173
Fat: 4g
Carbohydrate: 15g
Protein: 9g

INGREDIENTS

1 cup baby spinach leaves
1 stir bitter greens (arugula, dandelion, watercress, etc.)
1 cup sprouts
1 orange, into wedges
1/2 cup diced avocado
1/4 cup walnuts, soaked
2 tablespoons extra-virgin olive oil
1 tablespoon lemon juice
1 teaspoon lemon zest
Fresh cracked black pepper and salt to taste
1 tablespoon tahini
1/2 teaspoon diced fresh ginger

DIRECTIONS

1. Mix spinach leaves, bitter greens and sprouts in a bowl. Add the orange and avocado. In another bowl, whisk the lemon juice, olive oil, lemon zest, salt, pepper, ginger and tahini.
2. Pour the dressing over the salad and toss to coat. Trim with the chopped walnuts and serve immediately.

Chapter 8
Soups and Stews Recipes

Cannellini Bean Soup with Kale

PREPARATION TIME
15'

COOK TIME
25'

SERVING
5

NUTRITION

Calories: 188
Fat: 4.1g
Protein: 11.1g
Carbohydrates: 24.5g

INGREDIENTS

1 tablespoon olive oil
1/2 teaspoon ginger, minced
1/2 teaspoon cumin seeds
1 red onion, chopped
1 carrot, trimmed and chopped
1 parsnip, trimmed and chopped
2 garlic cloves, minced
5 cups vegetable broth
12 ounces Cannellini beans, drained
2 cups kale, torn into pieces
Sea salt and ground black pepper to taste

DIRECTIONS

1. In a heavy-bottomed pot, heat the olive over medium-high heat. Now, sauté the ginger and cumin for a minute or so.
2. Now, add in the onion, carrot and parsnip; continue sautéing an additional 3 minutes or until the vegetables are just tender.
3. Add in the garlic and continue to sauté for 1 minute or until aromatic.
4. Then pour in the vegetable broth and bring it to a boil. Immediately reduce the heat to a simmer and let it cook for 10 minutes.
5. Fold in the Cannellini beans and kale; continue to simmer until the kale wilts and everything is thoroughly heated. Season with salt and pepper to taste.
6. Ladle into individual bowls and serve hot. "Bon appétit!"

Coconut Watercress Soup

INGREDIENTS

1 teaspoon coconut oil
1 onion, diced
2 cups fresh or frozen peas
6 cups water, or vegetable stock
1 cup fresh watercress, chopped
1 tablespoon fresh mint, chopped
Pinch sea salt
Pinch freshly ground black pepper
¾ cup coconut milk

PREPARATION TIME
10'

COOK TIME
20'

SERVING
4

NUTRITION

Calories: 178
Fat: 10g
Protein: 6g
Carbohydrates: 18g

DIRECTIONS

1. Preparing the ingredients.
2. Melt the coconut oil in a large pot over medium-high heat. Add the onion and cook until soft for about 5 minutes, then add the peas and water. Bring to a boil, lower the heat, then add the watercress, mint, salt and pepper.
3. Cover and simmer for 5 minutes. Stir in the coconut milk.
4. Finish and serve.
5. Purée the soup until smooth in a blender or with an immersion blender.
6. Try this soup with any other fresh, leafy green, anything from spinach to collard greens to arugula to Swiss chard.

Easy Borscht

PREPARATION TIME
30'

COOK TIME
45'

SERVING
8

NUTRITION

Calories: 127
Fat: 0.3.g
Protein: 3.1g
Carbohydrates: 29.5g

INGREDIENTS

6 cups shredded red cabbage
2 large potatoes, peeled and chopped
1 cup peeled julienned beets
¼ cup chopped fresh parsley
2 cloves garlic, crushed
¼ cup red-wine vinegar
1 onion, chopped
5 teaspoons chopped fresh dill
2 tablespoons maple syrup (optional)
1 teaspoon paprika
Freshly ground pepper to taste
2 cups water
Fresh dill for garnish

DIRECTIONS

1. Combine all the ingredients in a large pot, except the dill.
2. Bring to a boil, cover, reduce the heat and cook over medium heat for 45 minutes.
3. Garnish with fresh dill and serve!

Potato and Corn Chowder

PREPARATION TIME
20'

COOK TIME
30'

SERVING
4

NUTRITION

Calories: 733
Fat: 8.5g
Carbohydrates: 148.5g
Protein: 20.4g

INGREDIENTS

2 tablespoons low-sodium vegetables broth
1 medium yellow onion, diced
1 stalk celery, diced
1 small red bell pepper, diced
2 teaspoons minced fresh thyme leaves (about 4 sprigs)
½ teaspoon smoked paprika
½ teaspoon no-salt-added Old Bay seasoning
1 jalapeno pepper, seeded and minced
1 clove garlic, minced
1 pound (454 grams) new potatoes, diced
3 cups fresh corn kernels (about 4 fresh cobs)
Salt to taste (optional)
Ground black or white pepper to taste
4 cups low-sodium vegetable broth
2 teaspoons white wine vinegar
Chopped chives for garnish

DIRECTIONS

1. Heat the vegetable broth in a large pot over medium heat. Add the onions and sauté for 4 minutes or until translucent.
2. Add the red bell pepper, celery, paprika, thyme, jalapeno and Old Bay seasoning. Sauté for 1 minute or until the vegetables are tender.
3. Add the garlic and sauté for another 1 minute or until fragrant.
4. Add the corn, potatoes, vegetable broth, salt (if desired) and pepper. Stir to mix well. Bring to a boil, then reduce the heat to low and simmer for 25 minutes or until the potatoes are soft.
5. Pour half of the soup in a blender, then process until the soup is creamy and smooth. Pour the puréed soup back to the pot and add the white wine vinegar. Stir to mix well.
6. Spread the chopped chives on top and serve.

Pumpkin Soup

PREPARATION TIME
20'

COOK TIME
1H 10'

SERVING
8

NUTRITION

Calories: 145
Fat: 8g
Carbohydrates: 16g
Protein: 3.5g

INGREDIENTS

3 pounds of quartered, seeded sugar pumpkin
3 cups of vegetable broth
2 chopped large shallots
3 chopped fresh sage leaves
1/4 cup of Greek yogurt
6 springs of thyme
1 tablespoon of grated ginger
1/8 teaspoon of nutmeg
1 teaspoon of sea salt
A pinch of ground pepper
1 (1/2) tablespoons of olive oil

DIRECTIONS

1. Preheat your oven to 450°F and spread some oil on a baking sheet.
2. Put pieces of pumpkin on the baking sheet. Drizzle them with olive oil and season with ground pepper and 1/4 teaspoon of sea salt. Put thyme sprigs on top.
3. Roast for about 1 hour, stirring halfway, and then let it cool and remove the skin.
4. Put a large stockpot on medium heat, pour olive oil and warm it. Add chopped shallots and cook for 5 minutes, stirring frequently, until tender.
5. Mix in vegetable broth, pumpkin, ginger and sage. Season with the remaining salt and ground pepper to taste.
6. Bring the mixture to a boil, then remove it from the heat.
7. Puree with a blender until smooth consistency, and then pour in Greek yogurt and blend repeatedly.
8. Serve with some Greek yogurt and enjoy!

Cannellini Pesto Spaghetti

PREPARATION TIME
5'

COOK TIME
10'

SERVING
4

INGREDIENTS

12 ounces whole-grain spaghetti, cooked, drained and kept warm, ½ cup cooking liquid reserved
1 cup pesto
2 cups cooked cannellini beans, drained and rinsed

DIRECTIONS

1. Put the cooked spaghetti in a large bowl and add the pesto.
2. Add the reserved cooking liquid and beans and toss well to serve.

NUTRITION

Calories: 549
Protein: 18.3g
Carbohydrates: 45g
Fats: 35g

Classic Tomato Soup

PREPARATION TIME
10'

COOK TIME
60'

SERVING
6

NUTRITION

Calories: 104
Fats: 0.8g
Carbohydrates: 23.4g
Protein: 4.3g

INGREDIENTS

3 pounds of halved tomatoes
1 cup of canned crushed tomatoes
2-3 chopped carrots
2 chopped yellow onions
5 minced garlic cloves
2 ounces of basil leaves
2 teaspoons of thyme leaves
1 teaspoon of dry oregano
½ teaspoon of ground cumin
½ teaspoon of paprika
2 (½) cups of water
Fresh lime juice to taste
2 tablespoons Extra virgin olive oil
Salt to taste
Black pepper to taste

DIRECTIONS

1. Preheat your oven to 450°F. Spread some oil inside a baking sheet.
2. Mix carrots with tomatoes in a large bowl. Add some oil, salt, black pepper and toss.
3. Put the vegetable mixture on the baking sheet in a single layer. Roast for 30 minutes, then set aside for 10 minutes.
4. Transfer the roasted vegetables to a food processor or a blender, add just a little water and blend.
5. Place a large stockpot on medium-high heat, pour 2 tablespoons of olive oil and warm it. Add chopped onions and simmer for 3 minutes, then add minced garlic and cook until golden.
6. Pour the blended mixture into the stockpot. Add in 2 (½) cups of water, canned tomatoes, thyme, basil and other seasonings. Bring it to a boil, reduce to low heat and cover. Simmer for about 20 minutes.
7. Serve with a splash of lime juice and enjoy!

Minestrone Soup

PREPARATION TIME
10'

COOK TIME
1H 5'

SERVING
6

NUTRITION

Calories: 298
Fat: 10.5g
Carbohydrates: 45.6g
Protein: 9.8g

INGREDIENTS

- 2 chopped carrots
- 2 chopped celeries (ribs)
- 1 chopped yellow onion
- 2 cups of chopped seasonal vegetables
- 2 cups of greens (chopped kale, spinach, collard greens)
- 4 cups of vegetable broth
- 1 can (28 ounces) of diced tomatoes with liquid
- 1 can (15 ounces) of canned beans
- 1 cup of the whole-grain small shell, elbow or orecchiette pasta
- ¼ cup of tomato paste
- 2 teaspoons of lemon juice
- 2 minced garlic cloves
- ½ teaspoon of thyme
- ½ teaspoon of oregano
- 2 bay leaves
- 1 teaspoon of sea salt
- 4 tablespoons of Extra virgin olive oil
- 2 cups of water
- A pinch of red pepper
- Black pepper to taste

DIRECTIONS

1. Place a large stockpot or Dutch oven on medium heat, pour 3 tablespoons of olive oil and warm. Add the chopped carrot, celery, onion, tomato paste and salt. Cook, stirring rapidly, for about 7-10 minutes until the vegetables are tender and onions become translucent.
2. Put in seasonal vegetables, thyme, oregano and garlic. Stir it and cook for 2 minutes until it smells fragrant.
3. Pour in vegetable broth, water and canned tomatoes with their liquid. Add in red pepper, bay leaves, black pepper with salt and stir it.
4. Increase to medium-high heat and bring it to a boil, then cover the pot with a lid, leaving a small 1-inch gap for steam escaping and reduce to low heat for simmering. Cook for 15 minutes.
5. Remove the lid and add beans, pasta and greens. Simmer for 20 minutes more until pasta is done.
6. Take it from the heat and remove bay leaves. Pour in 1 tablespoon of olive oil and lemon juice. Taste, add more seasonings if needed.
7. Serve and enjoy your Minestrone Soup.

Scallion and Mint Soup

INGREDIENTS

6 cups vegetable broth
¼ cup fresh mint leaves, roughly chopped
¼ cup chopped scallions, white and green parts
3 garlic cloves, minced
3 tablespoons freshly squeezed lime juice

PREPARATION TIME 5'

COOK TIME 15'

SERVING 4

DIRECTIONS

1. In a large stockpot, combine the broth, mint, scallions, garlic and lime juice. Bring to a boil over medium-high heat.
2. Cover, reduce the heat to low, simmer for 15 minutes and serve.

NUTRITION

Calories: 55
Protein: 5g
Carbohydrates: 5g
Fat: 2g

Green Pea Soup

PREPARATION TIME
5'

COOK TIME
50'

SERVING
6

NUTRITION

Calories: 297
Fat: 2g
Carbohydrates: 48g
Protein: 23g

INGREDIENTS

1 (16 ounces) package dried green split peas, soaked overnight
5 cups vegetable broth or water
2 teaspoons garlic powder
2 teaspoons onion powder
1 teaspoon dried oregano
1 teaspoon dried thyme
¼ teaspoon freshly ground black pepper

DIRECTIONS

1. In a large stockpot, combine the split peas, broth, garlic powder, onion powder, oregano, thyme and pepper. Bring to a boil over medium-high heat.
2. Cover, reduce the heat to medium-low and simmer for 45 minutes, stirring every 5 to 10 minutes. Serve warm.

Kale and Lentils Stew

INGREDIENTS

6 cups (2 pounds) brown or green dry lentils
8 cups vegetable broth or water
4 cups kale, stemmed and chopped into 2-inch pieces
2 large carrots, diced
1 tablespoon smoked paprika
2 teaspoons onion powder
2 teaspoons garlic powder
1 teaspoon red pepper flakes
1 teaspoon dried oregano
1 teaspoon dried thyme

PREPARATION TIME
10'

COOK TIME
50'

SERVING
8

NUTRITION

Calories: 467
Fat: 3g
Carbohydrates: 78g
Protein: 32g

DIRECTIONS

1. In a large stockpot, combine the lentils, broth, kale, carrots, paprika, onion powder, garlic powder, red pepper flakes, oregano and thyme. Bring to a boil over medium-high heat.
2. Cover, reduce the heat to medium-low and simmer for 45 minutes, stirring every 5 to 10 minutes. Serve warm.

Lentil Soup with Swiss Chard

PREPARATION TIME
10'

COOK TIME
25'

SERVING
5

NUTRITION

Calories: 148
Fat: 7.2g
Carbohydrates: 14.6g
Protein: 7.7g

INGREDIENTS

2 tablespoons olive oil
1 white onion, chopped
1 teaspoon garlic, minced
2 large carrots, chopped
1 parsnip, chopped
2 stalks celery, chopped
2 bay leaves
1/2 teaspoon dried thyme
1/4 teaspoon ground cumin
6 cups roasted vegetable broth
1 (1/4) cups brown lentils, soaked overnight and rinsed
2 cups Swiss chard, torn into pieces

DIRECTIONS

1. In a heavy-bottomed pot, heat the olive oil over moderate heat. Now, sauté the vegetables along with the spices for about 3 minutes until they are just tender.
2. Add in the vegetable broth and lentils, bringing it to a boil. Immediately turn the heat to a simmer and add in the bay leaves. Let it cook for about 15 minutes or until lentils are tender.
3. Add in the Swiss chard, cover and let it simmer for 5 minutes more or until the chard wilts.
4. Serve in individual bowls and enjoy!

Spicy Farro Soup

PREPARATION TIME
10'

COOK TIME
30'

SERVING
4

NUTRITION

Calories: 298
Fat: 8.9g
Protein: 11.7g
Carbohydrates: 44.6g

INGREDIENTS

2 tablespoons olive oil
1 medium-sized leek, chopped
1 medium-sized turnip, sliced
2 Italian peppers seeded and chopped
2 potatoes, peeled and diced
2 cups vegetable broth
1 cup farro, rinsed
1/2 teaspoon granulated garlic
1/2 teaspoon turmeric powder
1 bay laurel
2 cups spinach, turn into pieces

DIRECTIONS

1. In a heavy-bottomed pot, heat the olive oil over moderate heat. Now, sauté the leek, turnip, peppers and potatoes for about 5 minutes until they are crisp-tender.
2. Add in the vegetable broth, farro, granulated garlic, turmeric and bay laurel; bring it to a boil.
3. Immediately turn the heat to a simmer. Let it cook for about 25 minutes or until farro and potatoes have softened.
4. Add in the spinach and remove the pot from the heat; let the spinach sit in the residual heat until it wilts. "Bon appétit!"

Chickpea Noodle Soup

PREPARATION TIME
10'

COOK TIME
25'

SERVING
6

NUTRITION

Calories: 266
Total fat: 3g
Carbohydrates: 53g
Protein: 12g

INGREDIENTS

6 ounces dried soba noodles
4 cups vegetable broth, divided
2 cups diced onions
1 cup chopped carrots
1 cup chopped celery
3 garlic cloves, finely diced
½ teaspoon dried parsley
½ teaspoon dried sage
½ teaspoon dried thyme
½ teaspoon freshly ground black or white pepper
1 (15 ounces) can chickpeas, drained and rinsed
¼ cup chopped fresh parsley for garnish (optional)

DIRECTIONS

1. In a large saucepan, bring 4 cups of water to a boil over high heat. Add the soba noodles and cook, stirring occasionally, until just tender, 4 to 5 minutes. Drain in a colander and rinse well under cold water. Set aside.
2. In the same saucepan, heat ¼ cup of broth over medium-high heat. Add the onions, carrots, celery, garlic, parsley, sage, thyme and pepper and sauté for 5 minutes, or until the carrots are fork-tender.
3. Add the chickpeas and the remaining 3¾ cups of broth and bring to a boil. Lower the heat to low, cover and simmer for 15 minutes.
4. Serve garnished with parsley, if desired.

Greens and Grains Soup

PREPARATION TIME
5'

COOK TIME
35'

SERVING
6

NUTRITION

Calories: 183
Protein: 9g
Carbohydrates: 38g
Fats: 1g

INGREDIENTS

2 cups sliced onions
1 cup diced carrots
1 cup diced celery
1 cup dry farro
1 teaspoon dried basil
1 teaspoon dried oregano
½ teaspoon dried rosemary
½ teaspoon dried thyme
1 (15 ounces) can of diced tomatoes
1 (15 ounces) can of white kidney beans, drained and rinsed
6 ounces arugula
2 tablespoons lemon juice
4 cups water

DIRECTIONS

1. In a large saucepan, combine the onions, carrots and celery and dry sauté over medium-high heat, stirring occasionally until the carrots are softened about 5 minutes.
2. Add the farro and stir until coated. Add the basil, oregano, rosemary, thyme and 4 cups water and bring to a boil. Lower the heat to low, cover and simmer for 30 minutes.
3. Add the tomatoes and beans, raise the heat to medium-high and bring back to a boil.
4. Add the arugula and lemon juice and cook, stirring, until the arugula is a deep green and slightly wilted, 1 to 2 minutes more.
5. Remove from the heat and serve.

Vegan Pho

PREPARATION TIME
10'

COOK TIME
15'

SERVING
6

NUTRITION

Calories: 31
Fats: 0g
Carbohydrates: 7g
Protein: 2g

INGREDIENTS

1 package of wide rice noodles, cooked
1 medium white onion, peeled, quartered
2 teaspoons minced garlic
1-inch of ginger, sliced into coins
8 cups vegetable broth
1 whole clove
2 tablespoons soy sauce
1 whole star anise
1 cinnamon stick
3 cups of water

FOR TOPPINGS:
Basil as needed for topping
Chopped green onions as needed for topping
Ming beans as needed for topping
Hot sauce as needed for topping
Lime wedges for serving

DIRECTIONS

1. Take a large pot, place it over medium-high heat, add all the ingredients for soup in it, except for soy sauce and broth and bring it to boil.
2. Then switch heat to medium-low level, simmer the soup for 30 minutes and then stir in soy sauce.
3. When done, distribute cooked noodles into bowls, top with soup, then top with toppings and serve.

Creamy Spinach Rotini Soup

INGREDIENTS

1 teaspoon extra-virgin olive oil
1 cup chopped mushrooms
¼ teaspoon plus a pinch of salt
4 garlic cloves, minced, or 1 teaspoon garlic powder
2 peeled carrots or ½ red bell pepper, chopped
6 cups vegetable broth or water
Pinch freshly ground black pepper
1 cup rotini or gnocchi
¾ cup unsweetened nondairy milk
¼ cup nutritional yeast
2 cups chopped fresh spinach
¼ cup pitted black olives or sun-dried tomatoes, chopped
Herbed croutons for topping (optional)

DIRECTIONS

1. Heat the olive oil in a large soup pot over medium-high heat.
2. Add the mushrooms and a pinch of salt. Sauté for about 4 minutes until the mushrooms soften. Add the garlic (if using fresh) and carrots, then sauté for 1 minute. Add the vegetable broth, then add the remaining ¼ teaspoon of salt and pepper (plus the garlic powder if using). Bring to a boil and add the pasta. Cook for about 10 minutes until the pasta is cooked.
3. Finish and serve.
4. Turn off the heat and stir in the milk, nutritional yeast, spinach and olives. Top with croutons (if using). Leftovers will keep in an airtight container for up to 1 week in the refrigerator, or up to 1 month in the freezer.

PREPARATION TIME 5'

COOK TIME 15'

SERVING 4

NUTRITION

Calories: 207
Fat: 5g
Carbohydrates: 34g
Protein: 11g

Hot and Sour Tofu Soup

PREPARATION TIME
10'

COOK TIME
15'

SERVING
3

NUTRITION

Calories: 161
Protein: 13g
Carbohydrates: 10g
Fat: 9g

INGREDIENTS

6 to 7 ounces firm or extra-firm tofu
1 teaspoon Extra-virgin olive oil
1 cup sliced mushrooms
1 cup finely chopped cabbage
1 garlic clove, minced
½-inch piece fresh ginger, peeled and minced
Salt to taste
4 cups water or vegetable broth
2 tablespoons rice vinegar or apple cider vinegar
2 tablespoons soy sauce
1 teaspoon toasted sesame oil
1 teaspoon sugar
Pinch red pepper flakes to taste
1 scallion, white and light green parts only, chopped

DIRECTIONS

1. Press your tofu before you start. Put it between several layers of paper towels and place a heavy pan or book (with a waterproof cover or protected with plastic wrap) on top. Let it stand for 30 minutes. Discard the paper towels. Cut the tofu into ½-inch cubes.
2. In a large soup pot, heat the olive oil over medium-high heat.
3. Add the mushrooms, cabbage, garlic, ginger and a pinch of salt. Sauté for 7 to 8 minutes until the vegetables are softened.
4. Add the water, vinegar, soy sauce, sesame oil, sugar, red pepper flakes and tofu.
5. Bring to a boil, then turn the heat to low.
6. Finish and serve.
7. Simmer the soup for 5 to 10 minutes.
8. Serve with the scallion sprinkled on the top.

Winter Quinoa Soup

PREPARATION TIME 10'

COOK TIME 25'

SERVING 4

NUTRITION

Calories: 328
Fat: 11.1g
Carbohydrates: 44g
Protein: 13.3g

INGREDIENTS

2 tablespoons olive oil
1 onion, chopped
2 carrots, peeled and chopped
1 parsnip, chopped
1 celery stalk, chopped
1 cup yellow squash, chopped
4 garlic cloves, pressed or minced
4 cups roasted vegetable broth
2 medium tomatoes, crushed
1 cup quinoa
Sea salt and ground black pepper to taste
1 bay laurel
2 cups Swiss chard, tough ribs removed and torn into pieces
2 tablespoons Italian parsley, chopped

DIRECTIONS

1. In a heavy-bottomed pot, heat the olive over medium-high heat. Now, sauté the onion, carrot, parsnip, celery and yellow squash for about 3 minutes or until the vegetables are just tender.
2. Add in the garlic and continue to sauté for 1 minute or until aromatic.
3. Then, stir in the vegetable broth, tomatoes, quinoa, salt, pepper and bay laurel; bring to a boil. Immediately reduce the heat to a simmer and let it cook for 1 minutes.
4. Fold in the Swiss chard; continue to simmer until the chard wilts.
5. Ladle into individual bowls and serve garnished with the fresh parsley. "Bon appétit!"

CHAPTER 9
Pasta and Noodles Recipes

Stir-Fry Noodles

PREPARATION TIME
10'

COOK TIME
8'

SERVING
4

NUTRITION

Calories: 567
Total fat: 48g
Total carbs: 6g
Fiber: 4g
Net Carbs: 2g
Sodium: 373mg
Protein: 33g

INGREDIENTS

1 cup broccoli, chopped
1 cup red bell pepper, chopped
1 cup mushrooms, chopped
1 large onion, chopped
1 batch stir-fry sauce, prepared
Salt and black pepper to taste
2 cups spaghetti, cooked
4 garlic cloves, minced
2 tablespoons sesame oil

DIRECTIONS

1. Heat sesame oil in a pan over medium heat and add garlic, onions, bell pepper, broccoli, mushrooms.
2. Sauté for about 5 minutes and add spaghetti noodles and stir-fry sauce.
3. Mix well and cook for 3 more minutes.
4. Dish out in plates and serve to enjoy.

Spicy Sweet Chili Veggie Noodles

PREPARATION TIME
10'

COOK TIME
7'

SERVING
2

NUTRITION

Calories: 351
Total fat: 27g
Protein: 25g
Total carbs: 2g
Fiber: 1g
Net carbs: 1g

INGREDIENTS

1 head of broccoli, cut into bite-sized florets
1 onion, finely sliced
1 tablespoon olive oil
1 courgette, halved
2 nests of whole-wheat noodles
150 grams mushrooms, sliced

FOR SAUCE:
3 tablespoons soy sauce
¼ cup sweet chili sauce
1 teaspoon Sriracha
1 tablespoon peanut butter
2 tablespoons boiled water

FOR TOPPING:
2 teaspoons sesame seeds
2 teaspoons dried chili flakes

DIRECTIONS

1. Heat olive oil on medium heat in a saucepan and add onions.
2. Sauté for about 2 minutes and add broccoli, courgette and mushrooms.
3. Cook for about 5 minutes, stirring occasionally.
4. Whisk sweet chili sauce, soy sauce, Sriracha, water and peanut butter in a bowl.
5. Cook the noodles according to packet instructions and add to the vegetables.
6. Stir in the sauce and top with dried chili flakes and sesame seeds to serve.

Creamy Vegan Mushroom Pasta

PREPARATION TIME
10'

COOK TIME
30'

SERVING
6

NUTRITION

Calories: 364
Total fat: 28g
Protein: 24g
Total carbs: 4g
Fiber: 2g
Net carbs: 2g

INGREDIENTS

2 cups frozen peas, thawed
3 tablespoons flour, unbleached
3 cups almond beverage, unsweetened
1 tablespoon nutritional yeast
1/3 cup fresh parsley, chopped, plus extra for garnish
1/4 cup olive oil
1 pound pasta of choice
4 cloves garlic, minced
2/3 cup shallots, chopped
8 cups mixed mushrooms, sliced
Salt and black pepper to taste

DIRECTIONS

1. Take a bowl and boil pasta in salted water.
2. Heat olive oil in a pan over medium heat.
3. Add mushrooms, garlic, shallots and ½ teaspoon salt and cook for 15 minutes.
4. Sprinkle flour on the vegetables and stir for a minute while cooking.
5. Add almond beverage, stir constantly.
6. Let it simmer for 5 minutes and add pepper to it.
7. Cook for 3 more minutes and remove from heat.
8. Stir in nutritional yeast.
9. Add peas, salt and pepper.
10. Cook for another minute.
11. Add pasta to this sauce.
12. Garnish and serve!

Vegan Chinese Noodles

PREPARATION TIME
15'

COOK TIME
8'

SERVING
4

NUTRITION

Calories: 314
Total fat: 22g
Protein: 26g
Total carbs: 3g
Fiber: 0.3g
Net carbs: 2.7g

INGREDIENTS

- 300 grams mixed oriental mushrooms, such as oyster, shiitake and enoki, cleaned and sliced
- 200 grams thin rice noodles, cooked according to packet instructions and drained
- 2 garlic cloves, minced
- 1 fresh red chili
- 200 grams courgettes, sliced
- 6 spring onions, reserving the green part
- 1 teaspoon cornflour
- 1 tablespoon agave syrup
- 1 teaspoon sesame oil
- 100 grams baby spinach, chopped
- Hot chili sauce to serve
- 2 (1-inch) pieces of ginger
- ½ bunch fresh coriander, chopped
- 4 tablespoons vegetable oil
- 2 tablespoons low-salt soy sauce
- ½ tablespoon rice wine
- 2 limes to serve
- 2 tablespoons water

DIRECTIONS

1. Heat sesame oil over high heat in a large wok and add the mushrooms.
2. Sauté for about 4 minutes and add garlic, chili, ginger, courgette, coriander stalks and the white part of the spring onions.
3. Sauté for about 3 minutes until softened and lightly golden.
4. Meanwhile, combine the cornflour and 2 tablespoons of water in a bowl.
5. Add soy sauce, agave syrup, sesame oil and rice wine to the cornflour mixture.
6. Put this mixture in the pan to the veggie mixture and cook for about 3 minutes until thickened.
7. Add the spinach and noodles and mix well.
8. Stir in the coriander leaves and top with lime wedges, hot chili sauce and reserved spring onions to serve.

Vegetable Penne Pasta

PREPARATION TIME
15'

COOK TIME
20'

SERVING
6

NUTRITION

Calories: 385
Total fat: 29g
Protein: 26g
Total carbs: 5g
Fiber: 1g
Net carbs: 4g

INGREDIENTS

½ large onion, chopped
2 celery sticks, chopped
½ tablespoon ginger paste
½ cup green bell pepper
1 (½) tablespoons soy sauce
½ teaspoon parsley
Salt and black pepper to taste
½ pound penne pasta, cooked
2 large carrots, diced
½ small leek, chopped
1 tablespoon olive oil
½ teaspoon garlic paste
½ tablespoon Worcester sauce
½ teaspoon coriander
1 cup water

DIRECTIONS

1. Heat olive oil in a wok on medium heat and add onions, garlic and ginger paste.
2. Sauté for about 3 minutes and stir in all bell pepper, celery sticks, carrots and leek.
3. Sauté for about 5 minutes and add the remaining ingredients except for pasta.
4. Cover the lid and cook for about 12 minutes.
5. Stir in the cooked pasta and dish out to serve warm.

Spaghetti in Spicy Tomato Sauce

PREPARATION TIME
15'

COOK TIME
40'

SERVING
4

NUTRITION

Calories: 313
Total fat: 25g
Protein: 21g
Total carbs: 1g
Fiber: 0g
Net carbs: 1g

INGREDIENTS

1 pound dried spaghetti
1 red bell pepper, diced
4 garlic cloves, minced
1 teaspoon red pepper flakes, crushed
2 (14 ounces) cans of diced tomatoes
1 (6 ounces) can tomato paste
2 teaspoons vegan sugar, granulated
2 tablespoons olive oil
1 medium onion, diced
1 cup dry red wine
1 teaspoon dried thyme
½ teaspoon fennel seed, crushed
1 (½) cups coconut milk, full-fat
Salt and black pepper to taste

DIRECTIONS

1. Boil water in a large pot and add pasta.
2. Cook according to the package directions and drain the pasta into a colander.
3. Dish out the pasta in a large serving bowl and add a dash of olive oil to prevent sticking.
4. Heat 2 tablespoons of olive oil over medium heat in a large pot and add garlic, onion and bell pepper.
5. Sauté for about 5 minutes and stir in the wine, thyme, fennel and red pepper flakes.
6. Allow simmering on high heat for about 5 minutes until the liquid is reduced by about half.
7. Add diced tomatoes and tomato paste and allow to simmer for about 20 minutes, stirring occasionally.
8. Stir in the coconut milk and sugar and simmer for about 10 more minutes.
9. Season with salt and black pepper and pour the sauce over the pasta.
10. Toss to coat well and dish out in plates to serve.

20 Minutes Vegetarian Pasta

PREPARATION TIME
5'

COOK TIME
16'

SERVING
4

NUTRITION

Calories: 284
Total fat: 18g
Protein: 29g
Total carbs: 1.5g
Fiber: 0g
Net carbs: 1.5g

INGREDIENTS

3 shallots, chopped
¼ teaspoon red pepper flakes
¼ cup vegan parmesan cheese
2 tablespoons olive oil
2 garlic cloves, minced
8 ounces spinach leaves
8 ounces linguine pasta
1 pinch salt
1 pinch black pepper

DIRECTIONS

1. Boil salted water in a large pot and add pasta.
2. Cook for about 6 minutes and drain the pasta in a colander.
3. Heat olive oil over medium heat in a large skillet and add the shallots.
4. Cook for about 5 minutes until soft and caramelized and stir in the spinach, garlic, red pepper flakes, salt and black pepper.
5. Cook for about 5 minutes and add pasta and 2 ladles of pasta water.
6. Stir in the parmesan cheese and dish out in a bowl to serve.

Creamy Vegan Pumpkin Pasta

PREPARATION TIME
15'

COOK TIME
5'

SERVING
6

NUTRITION

Calories: 431
Total fat: 31g
Protein: 35g
Total carbs: 3g
Fiber: 0.5g
Net carbs: 2.5g

INGREDIENTS

1 tablespoon olive oil
1 cup raw cashews, soaked in water 4-8 hours, drained and rinsed
12 ounces dried penne pasta
1 cup pumpkin puree, canned
1 cup almond milk, plus more as needed
3 garlic cloves
¼ teaspoon ground nutmeg
Fresh parsley for garnish
1 tablespoon lemon juice
¾ teaspoon salt
1 tablespoon fresh sage, chopped

DIRECTIONS

1. Boil salted water in a large pot and add pasta.
2. Cook according to the package directions and drain the pasta into a colander.
3. Dish out the pasta in a large serving bowl and add a dash of olive oil to prevent sticking.
4. Put the pumpkin, cashews, milk, lemon juice, garlic, salt and nutmeg into the food processor and blend until smooth.
5. Stir in the sauce and sage over the pasta and toss to coat well.
6. Garnish with fresh parsley and dish out to serve hot.

Loaded Creamy Vegan Pesto Pasta

PREPARATION TIME
15'

COOK TIME
10'

SERVING
6

NUTRITION

Calories: 220
Total fat: 10g
Protein: 31g
Total carbs: 1.5g
Fiber: 0.5g
Net carbs: 1g

INGREDIENTS

¼ onion, finely chopped
8 romaine lettuce leaves
1 celery stalk, thinly sliced
½ cup blue cheese, crumbled
1 tablespoon olive oil, plus a dash
1 cup almond milk, unflavored and unsweetened
½ cup vegan pesto
1 cup chickpeas, cooked
1 cup fresh arugula, packed
2 tablespoons lemon juice
Salt and black pepper to taste
6 ounces orecchiette pasta, dried
1 cup full-fat coconut milk
2 tablespoons whole wheat flour
1 (½) cups cherry tomatoes halved
½ cup Kalamata olives halved
Red pepper flakes to taste

DIRECTIONS

1. Boil salted water in a large pot and add pasta.
2. Cook according to the package directions and drain the pasta into a colander.
3. Dish out the pasta in a large serving bowl and add a dash of olive oil to prevent sticking.
4. Put olive oil over medium heat in a large pot and whisk in the flour.
5. Cook for about 4 minutes, until the mixture begins to smell nutty and stir in the coconut milk and almond milk.
6. Let the sauce simmer for about 1 minute and add the chickpeas, olives and arugula.
7. Stir well and season with lemon juice, red pepper flakes, salt and black pepper.
8. Dish out onto plates and serve hot.

Creamy Vegan Spinach Pasta

PREPARATION TIME
20'

COOK TIME
5'

SERVING
4

NUTRITION

Calories: 94
Total fat: 10g
Protein: 0g
Total carbs: 1g
Fiber: 0.3g
Net carbs: 0.7g

INGREDIENTS

1 cup raw cashews, soaked in water for 8 hours
2 tablespoons lemon juice
1 tablespoon olive oil
1 (½) cups vegetable broth
2 tablespoons fresh dill, chopped
Red pepper flakes to taste
10 ounces dried fusilli
½ cup almond milk, unflavored and unsweetened
2 tablespoons white miso paste
4 garlic cloves, divided
8 ounces fresh spinach, finely chopped
¼ cup scallions, chopped
Salt and black pepper to taste

DIRECTIONS

1. Boil salted water in a large pot and add pasta.
2. Cook according to the package directions and drain the pasta into a colander.
3. Dish out the pasta in a large serving bowl and add a dash of olive oil to prevent sticking.
4. Put the cashews, milk, miso, lemon juice and 1 garlic clove into the food processor and blend until smooth.
5. Put olive oil over medium heat in a large pot and add the remaining 3 cloves of garlic.
6. Sauté for about 1 minute and stir in the spinach and broth.
7. Raise the heat and allow to simmer for about 4 minutes until the spinach is bright green and wilted.
8. Stir in the pasta and cashew mixture and season with salt and black pepper.
9. Top with scallions and dill, and dish out onto plates to serve.

Chapter 10
Homemade Sauces and Condiments Recipes

Catalina Dressing

PREPARATION TIME
5'

COOK TIME
0'

SERVING
2

NUTRITION

Calories: 47
Fat: 4.3g
Fiber: 1.5g
Carbs: 2.4g
Protein: 2.4g

INGREDIENTS

1/2 teaspoon dry mustard
1/2 teaspoon chili powder
1/2 teaspoon onion powder
3 tablespoons apple cider vinegar
1/4 cup olive oil
1/4 cup tomato sauce

DIRECTIONS

1. Mix well all the ingredients and store in the refrigerator.

Coleslaw Dressing

INGREDIENTS

1 teaspoon celery seed,
1 teaspoon onion powder
1 tablespoon agave nectar
1 tablespoon Dijon mustard
2 tablespoons apple cider vinegar
1/2 cup veganize (vegan mayo)

PREPARATION TIME
5'

COOK TIME
0'

SERVING
12

NUTRITION

Calories: 47
Fat: 0.3g
Fiber: 1.5g
Carbs: 0.4g
Protein: 0.4g

DIRECTIONS

1. Mix well all the ingredients and store in the refrigerator.

Walnut Basil Dressing

PREPARATION TIME
10'

COOK TIME
0'

SERVING
2

NUTRITION

Calories: 89
Fat: 0.3g
Fiber: 1.5g
Carbs: 0.4g
Protein: 0.4g

INGREDIENTS

2 to 4 tablespoons water, as needed
¼ teaspoon salt
1 tablespoon garlic, minced
3 tablespoons lemon juice
¼ cup nutritional yeast
¼ cup olive oil
½ cup walnuts, crushed
1 cup basil leaves packed loosely, chopped fine

DIRECTIONS

1. Mix all the ingredients in a food processor or blender until smooth. Add spoons of water as needed to maintain a thick but workable consistency.
2. The finished product should resemble a pesto sauce.

Moroccan Carrot Dip

PREPARATION TIME
15'

COOK TIME
0'

SERVING
1

NUTRITION

Calories: 110
Fat: 0.3g
Fiber: 1.5g
Carbs: 0.4g
Protein: 0.4g

INGREDIENTS

1/2 cup water
1/4 teaspoon black pepper
1/2 teaspoon salt
1/4 teaspoon fennel
1/2 teaspoon coriander, ground
1/2 teaspoon cumin, ground
1 teaspoon cinnamon
1 teaspoon ginger, ground
1 tablespoon garlic, minced
2 teaspoons apple cider vinegar
1/3 cup cashews, raw
1 cup carrot, raw, cut into small chunks

DIRECTIONS

1. Puree all the listed ingredients until everything is smooth and creamy.

Tahini Citrus Dressing

INGREDIENTS

½ teaspoon black pepper
½ teaspoon salt
1 tablespoon garlic, minced
1 teaspoon ginger, ground
2 teaspoons Dijon mustard
2 tablespoons agave nectar
1 tablespoon apple cider vinegar
2 tablespoons tahini
1 tablespoon lemon juice
3 tablespoons orange juice

PREPARATION TIME
15'

COOK TIME
0

SERVING
8

DIRECTIONS

1. Mix all the ingredients that are listed in a blender until they are creamy and smooth.

NUTRITION

Calories: 98
Fat: 0.3g
Fiber: 1.5g
Carbs: 0.4g
Protein: 0.4g

Curried Almond Dressing

PREPARATION TIME
15'

COOK TIME
0'

SERVING
8

NUTRITION

Calories: 85
Fat: 0.3g
Fiber: 1.5g
Carbs: 0.4g
Protein: 0.4g

INGREDIENTS

1/8 teaspoon curry powder
1/8 teaspoon black pepper
1/2 teaspoon salt
1/2 teaspoon Dijon mustard
1 teaspoon ginger, ground
1 tablespoon garlic, minced
2/3 cup water
2 tablespoons agave nectar
2 tablespoons apple cider vinegar
1/2 cup almonds, raw

DIRECTIONS

1. Puree well all the ingredients in a blender until they are creamy and smooth.

Applesauce Salad Dressing

PREPARATION TIME
5'

COOK TIME
0'

SERVING
12

NUTRITION

Calories: 105
Fat: 0.3g
Fiber: 1.5g
Carbs: 0.4g
Protein: 0.4g

INGREDIENTS

1/8 teaspoon black pepper
1/4 teaspoon salt
1 teaspoon cinnamon
1/4 teaspoon cumin
1 teaspoon Dijon mustard
1 teaspoon chickpea miso
1 tablespoon balsamic vinegar
2 tablespoons apple cider vinegar
1/2 cup applesauce, unsweetened

DIRECTIONS

1. Mix well all the ingredients in a blender.

Balsamic Vinaigrette

PREPARATION TIME
5'

COOK TIME
0'

SERVING
8

NUTRITION

Calories: 91
Fat: 0.3g
Fiber: 1.5g
Carbs: 0.4g
Protein: 0.4g

INGREDIENTS

¼ teaspoon black pepper
¼ teaspoon salt
¼ teaspoon garlic powder
1 tablespoon agave nectar
1 tablespoon Dijon mustard
¼ cup balsamic vinegar
½ cup olive oil

DIRECTIONS

1. Mix well all the ingredients in a blender or in a shaker jar.

Chipotle Lime Dressing

INGREDIENTS

¼ teaspoon garlic powder
¼ teaspoon paprika
1 tablespoon agave nectar
1 red pepper, chopped
3 tablespoons lime juice
3 tablespoons veganize

PREPARATION TIME
5'

COOK TIME
0'

SERVING
8

DIRECTIONS

1. Mix well all the ingredients in a shaker jar or in a blender.

NUTRITION

Calories: 32
Fat: 0.3g
Fiber: 1.5g
Carbs: 0.4g
Protein: 0.4g

White Beans Dip

PREPARATION TIME
15'

COOK TIME
15'

SERVING
6

NUTRITION

Calories: 263
Total fat: 18.1g
Saturated fat: 2.5g
Cholesterol: 0mg
Sodium: 630mg
Total Carbs: 20.2g
Fiber: 5.7g
Sugar: 0.3g
Protein: 7g

INGREDIENTS

1/2 cup olive oil
2 tablespoons garlic cloves, chopped
2 (15.8 ounces) cans of white beans, drained and rinsed
1/4 cup fresh lemon juice
4 tablespoons fresh parsley, chopped and divided
1 teaspoon ground cumin
1/4 tablespoon salt
1 teaspoon ground white pepper

DIRECTIONS

1. In a small saucepan, place the olive oil and garlic over medium-low heat and cook for about 2 minutes, stirring continuously.
2. Remove the pan of garlic oil from heat and let it cool slightly.
3. Strain the garlic oil, reserving both the oil and garlic in separate bowls.
4. In a food processor, place the beans, garlic, lemon juice, 2 tablespoons of parsley and cumin, and pulse until smooth.
5. While the motor is running, add the reserved oil and pulse until light and smooth.
6. Transfer the dip into a bowl and stir in salt and white pepper.
7. Serve with the garnishing of the remaining parsley.

Edamame Hummus

PREPARATION TIME
15'

COOK TIME
11'

SERVING
5

NUTRITION

Calories: 339
Total Fat: 33.8g
Saturated Fat: 4.3g
Cholesterol: 0mg
Sodium: 27mg

INGREDIENTS

10 ounces frozen edamame pods
1 ripe avocado, peeled, pitted and chopped roughly
1/2 cup fresh cilantro, chopped
1/4 cup scallion, chopped
1 jalapeno pepper
1 garlic clove, peeled
2-3 tablespoons fresh lime juice
Salt and ground black pepper to taste
1/4 cup avocado oil
2 tablespoons fresh basil leaves

DIRECTIONS

1. In a small pot of boiling water, cook the edamame pods for 6-8 minutes.
2. Drain the edamame pods and let them cool completely.
3. Remove soybeans from the pods.
4. In a food processor, add edamame and the remaining ingredients (except for oil) and pulse until mostly pureed.
5. While the motor is running, add the reserved oil and pulse until light and smooth.
6. Transfer the hummus into a bowl and serve with the garnishing of the remaining basil leaves.

Beans Mayonnaise

PREPARATION TIME
10'

COOK TIME
2'

SERVING
4

NUTRITION

Calories: 8
Total fat: 1.1g
Saturated fat: 0.1g
Cholesterol: 0mg
Sodium: 559mg

INGREDIENTS

1 (15 ounces) can of white beans, drained and rinsed
2 tablespoons apple cider vinegar
1 tablespoon fresh lemon juice
2 tablespoons yellow mustard
3/4 teaspoon salt
2 garlic cloves, peeled
2 tablespoons aquafaba (liquid from the can of beans)

DIRECTIONS

1. In a food processor, add all ingredients (except for oil) and pulse until mostly pureed.
2. While the motor is running, add the reserved oil and pulse until light and smooth.
3. Transfer the mayonnaise into a container and refrigerate to chill before serving.

CASHEW CREAM

PREPARATION TIME
10'

COOK TIME
0'

SERVING
5

NUTRITION

Calories: 165
Total fat: 12.8g
Saturated fat: 2.5g
Cholesterol: 0mg
Sodium: 65mg
Total carbs: 9.9g

INGREDIENTS

1 cup raw, unsalted cashews, soaked for 12 hours and drained
1/2 cup water
1 tablespoon nutritional yeast
1 teaspoon fresh lemon juice
1/8 teaspoon salt

DIRECTIONS

1. In a food processor, add all ingredients and pulse at high speed until creamy and smooth.
2. Serve immediately.

Lemon Tahini

INGREDIENTS

1/4 cup fresh lemon juice
4 medium garlic cloves, pressed
1/2 cup tahini
1/2 teaspoon fine sea salt
A pinch of ground cumin
6 tablespoons ice water

PREPARATION TIME
15'

COOK TIME
0'

SERVING
4

NUTRITION

Calories: 187
Total fat: 16.3g
Saturated fat: 2.4g
Cholesterol: 0mg
Sodium: 273mg

DIRECTIONS

1. In a medium bowl, combine the lemon juice and garlic and set aside for 10 minutes.
2. Through a fine-mesh sieve, strain the mixture into another medium bowl, pressing the garlic solids.
3. Discard the garlic solids.
4. In the bowl of lemon juice, add the tahini, salt and cumin, and whisk until well blended.
5. Slowly, add water, 2 tablespoons at a time, whisking well after each addition.

Keto-Vegan Ketchup

PREPARATION TIME
35'

COOK TIME
11'

SERVING
12

NUTRITION

Calories: 13
Carbohydrates: 2g
Proteins: 0g
Fats: 0g

INGREDIENTS

1/8 teaspoon mustard powder
1/8 teaspoon cloves, ground
1/4 teaspoon paprika
1/2 teaspoon garlic powder
3/4 teaspoon onion powder
1 teaspoon sea salt
1 tablespoon apple cider vinegar
1/4 cup powdered monk fruit
1 cup water
6 ounces tomato paste

DIRECTIONS

1. In a little saucepan, whisk together all the ingredients.
2. Cover the pan and bring to low heat and simmer for 30 minutes, stirring occasionally.
3. Once reduced, add to the blender and puree until it's a smooth consistency.

Avocado Hummus

PREPARATION TIME
5'

COOK TIME
5'

SERVING
6

NUTRITION

Calories: 310
Carbohydrates: 26g
Proteins: 8g
Fats: 20g

INGREDIENTS

1/8 teaspoon cumin
1 clove garlic
3 tablespoons lime juice
1 (1/2) tablespoons tahini
1 (1/2) tablespoons olive oil
2 avocados, medium cored & peeled
15 ounces chickpeas, drained
Salt and pepper to taste

DIRECTIONS

1. In a food processor, add garlic, lime juice, tahini, olive oil and chickpeas, and pulse until combined.
2. Add cumin and avocados, and blend until smooth consistency approximately 2 minutes.
3. Add salt and pepper to taste.

Guacamole

PREPARATION TIME
5'

COOK TIME
5'

SERVING
6

NUTRITION

Calories: 127
Carbohydrates: 9.3g
Proteins: 2.4g
Fats: 10.2g

INGREDIENTS

3 tablespoons tomato, diced
3 tablespoons onion, diced
2 tablespoons cilantro, chopped
2 tablespoons jalapeno juice
1/4 teaspoon garlic powder
1/2 teaspoon salt
1/2 lime, squeezed
2 big avocados
1 jalapeno, diced

DIRECTIONS

1. Using a molcajete, crush the diced jalapenos until soft.
2. Add the avocados to the molcajete.
3. Squeeze the lime juice from ½ of the lime on top of the avocados.
4. Add the jalapeno juice, garlic and salt, and mix until smooth.
5. Once smooth, add in the onion, cilantro and tomato, and stir to incorporate.

Keto-Vegan Mayo

PREPARATION TIME
5'

COOK TIME
5'

SERVING
6

NUTRITION

Calories: 160.4
Carbohydrates: 0.2g
Proteins: 0g
Fats: 18g

INGREDIENTS

1/2 cup Extra virgin olive oil
1/2 cup almond milk, unsweetened
1/4 teaspoon xanthan gum
A pinch of white pepper, ground
A pinch of Himalayan salt
1 teaspoon Dijon mustard
2 teaspoons apple cider vinegar

DIRECTIONS

1. In a blender, place milk, pepper, salt, mustard and vinegar.
2. Turn the blender to high speed and slowly add xanthan, then the olive oil.
3. Remove from the blender and allow cooling for 2 hours in the refrigerator.
4. During cooling, the mixture will thicken.

Peanut Sauce

INGREDIENTS

1/2 teaspoon Thai red curry paste
1 teaspoon coconut oil
1 teaspoon soy sauce
1 teaspoon chili garlic sauce
1 tablespoon sweetener of your choice
1/3 cup coconut milk
1/4 cup peanut butter, smooth

PREPARATION TIME
10'

COOK TIME
10'

SERVING
4

NUTRITION

Calories: 151
Carbohydrates: 4g
Proteins: 4g
Fats: 13g

DIRECTIONS

1. Using a microwave-safe dish, add the peanut butter and heat for about 30 seconds.
2. Whisk into the peanut butter soy sauce, sweetener and chili garlic, then set to the side.
3. Warm a little saucepan over medium heat and add oil.
4. Cook the Thai red curry paste until fragrant, then add to a microwave-safe bowl.
5. Continuously, stir the peanut mixture as you add the coconut milk. Stir until well-combined.
6. Enjoy at room temperature or warmed.

Pistachio Dip

INGREDIENTS

2 tablespoons lemon juice
1 teaspoon Extra virgin olive oil
2 tablespoons tahini
2 tablespoons parsley, chopped
2 cloves of garlic
1/2 cup pistachios shelled
15 ounces garbanzo beans, save the liquid from the can
Salt and pepper to taste

PREPARATION TIME
10'

COOK TIME
10'

SERVING
8

NUTRITION

Calories: 88
Carbohydrates: 9g
Proteins: 2.5g
Fats: 3g

DIRECTIONS

1. Using a food processor, add pistachios, pepper, sea salt, lemon juice, olive oil, tahini, parsley, garlic and garbanzo beans. Pulse until mixed.
2. Using the liquid from the garbanzo beans, add to the dip while slowly blending until it reaches your desired consistency.
3. Enjoy at room temperature or warmed.

Chapter 11
Rice and Grains Recipes

Classic Garlicky Rice

PREPARATION TIME
5'

COOK TIME
20'

SERVING
4

NUTRITION

Calories: 422
Fat: 15.1g
Carbs: 61.1g
Protein: 9.3g

INGREDIENTS

4 tablespoons olive oil
4 cloves garlic, chopped
½ cup white rice
½ cup vegetable broth

DIRECTIONS

1. In a saucepan, heat the olive oil over a moderately high flame. Add in the garlic and sauté for about 1 minute or until aromatic.
2. Add in the rice and broth. Bring to a boil; immediately turn the heat to a gentle simmer.
3. Cook for about 15 minutes or until all the liquid has been absorbed. Fluff the rice with a fork, season with salt and pepper and serve hot!

Brown Rice with Vegetables and Tofu

PREPARATION TIME
10'

COOK TIME
35'

SERVING
4

NUTRITION

Calories: 410
Fat: 13.2g
Carbs: 60g
Protein: 14.3g

INGREDIENTS

4 teaspoons sesame oil
2 spring garlic stalks, minced
1 cup spring onions, chopped
1 carrot, trimmed and sliced
1 celery rib, sliced
1/4 cup dry white wine
10 ounces tofu, cubed
1 (1/2) cups long-grain brown rice, rinsed thoroughly
2 tablespoons soy sauce
2 tablespoons tahini
1 tablespoon lemon juice
2 (1/2) cups water

DIRECTIONS

1. In a wok or large saucepan, heat 2 teaspoons of the sesame oil over medium-high heat. Now, cook the garlic, onion, carrot and celery for about 3 minutes, stirring periodically to ensure even cooking.
2. Add the wine to degrease the pan and push the vegetables to one side of the wok. Add in the remaining sesame oil and fry the tofu for 8 minutes, stirring occasionally.
3. Bring 2 (1/2) cups of water to a boil over medium-high heat. Bring to a simmer and cook the rice for about 30 minutes or until it is tender; fluff the rice and stir it with the soy sauce and tahini.
4. Stir the vegetables and tofu into the hot rice; add a few drizzles of the fresh lemon juice and serve warm. "Bon appétit!"

Basic Amaranth Porridge

PREPARATION TIME
10'

COOK TIME
35'

SERVING
4

NUTRITION

Calories: 261
Fat: 4.4g
Carbs: 49g
Protein: 7.3g

INGREDIENTS

3 cups water
1 cup amaranth
1/2 cup coconut milk
4 tablespoons agave syrup
A pinch of kosher salt
A pinch of grated nutmeg

DIRECTIONS

1. Bring the water to a boil over medium-high heat; add in the amaranth and turn the heat to a simmer.
2. Let it cook for about 30 minutes, stirring periodically to prevent the amaranth from sticking to the bottom of the pan.
3. Stir in the remaining ingredients and continue to cook for 1 to 2 minutes more until cooked through. "Bon appétit!"

COUNTRY CORNBREAD WITH SPINACH

PREPARATION TIME
10'

COOK TIME
40'

SERVING
8

NUTRITION

Calories: 282
Fat: 15.4g
Carbs: 30g
Protein: 4.6g

INGREDIENTS

1 tablespoon flaxseed meal
1 cup all-purpose flour
1 cup yellow cornmeal
½ teaspoon baking soda
½ teaspoon baking powder
1 teaspoon kosher salt
1 teaspoon brown sugar
A pinch of grated nutmeg
1 (¼) cups oat milk, unsweetened
1 teaspoon white vinegar
½ cup olive oil
2 cups spinach, torn into pieces
3 tablespoons water

DIRECTIONS

1. Start by preheating your oven to 420°F. Now, spritz a baking pan with a nonstick cooking spray.
2. To make the flax eggs, mix flaxseed meal with 3 tablespoons of water. Stir and let it sit for about 15 minutes.
3. In a mixing bowl, thoroughly combine the flour, cornmeal, baking soda, baking powder, salt, sugar and grated nutmeg.
4. Gradually add in the flax egg, oat milk, vinegar and olive oil, whisking constantly to avoid lumps. Afterward, fold in the spinach.
5. Scrap the batter into the prepared baking pan. Bake your cornbread for about 25 minutes or until a tester inserted in the middle comes out dry and clean.
6. Let it stand for about 10 minutes before slicing and serving. Bon appétit!

Rice Pudding with Currants

PREPARATION TIME
10'

COOK TIME
40'

SERVING
4

NUTRITION

Calories: 423
Fat: 5.3g
Carbs: 85g
Protein: 8.8g

INGREDIENTS

½ cup water
1 cup white rice
½ cup oat milk, divided
½ cup white sugar
A pinch of salt
A pinch of grated nutmeg
1 teaspoon ground cinnamon
½ teaspoon vanilla extract
½ cup dried currants

DIRECTIONS

1. In a saucepan, bring the water to a boil over medium-high heat. Immediately turn the heat to a simmer, add in the rice and let it cook for about 20 minutes.
2. Add in the milk, sugar and spices, and continue to cook for 20 minutes more, stirring constantly to prevent the rice from sticking to the pan.
3. Top with dried currants and serve at room temperature. "Bon appétit!"

Millet Porridge with Sultanas

PREPARATION TIME
5'

COOK TIME
30'

SERVING
3

NUTRITION

Calories: 353
Fat: 5.5g
Carbs: 65.2g
Protein: 9.8g

INGREDIENTS

1 cup water
1 cup coconut milk
1 cup millet, rinsed
1/4 teaspoon grated nutmeg
1/4 teaspoon ground cinnamon
1 teaspoon vanilla paste
1/4 teaspoon kosher salt
2 tablespoons agave syrup
4 tablespoons sultana raisins

DIRECTIONS

1. Place the water, milk, millet, nutmeg, cinnamon, vanilla and salt in a saucepan; bring to a boil.
2. Turn the heat to a simmer and let it cook for about 20 minutes; fluff the millet with a fork and spoon into individual bowls.
3. Serve with agave syrup and sultanas. "Bon appétit!"

Quinoa Porridge with Dried Figs

PREPARATION TIME
5'

COOK TIME
25'

SERVING
3

NUTRITION

Calories: 414
Fat: 9g
Carbs: 71.2g
Protein: 13.8g

INGREDIENTS

1 cup white quinoa, rinsed
2 cups almond milk
4 tablespoons brown sugar
A pinch of salt
1/4 teaspoon grated nutmeg
1/2 teaspoon ground cinnamon
1/2 teaspoon vanilla extract
1/2 cup dried figs, chopped

DIRECTIONS

1. Place the quinoa, almond milk, sugar, salt, nutmeg, cinnamon and vanilla extract in a saucepan.
2. Bring it to a boil over medium-high heat. Turn the heat to a simmer and let it cook for about 20 minutes; fluff with a fork.
3. Divide between three serving bowls and garnish with dried figs. "Bon appétit!"

Bread Pudding with Raisins

PREPARATION TIME
5'

COOK TIME
60'

SERVING
4

NUTRITION

Calories: 474
Fat: 12.2g
Carbs: 72g
Protein: 14.4g

INGREDIENTS

4 cups day-old bread, cubed
1 cup brown sugar
4 cups coconut milk
1/2 teaspoon vanilla extract
1 teaspoon ground cinnamon
2 tablespoons rum
1/2 cup raisins

DIRECTIONS

1. Start by preheating your oven to 360°F. Lightly oil a casserole dish with a nonstick cooking spray.
2. Place the cubed bread in the prepared casserole dish.
3. In a mixing bowl, thoroughly combine the sugar, milk, vanilla, cinnamon, rum and raisins. Pour the custard evenly over the bread cubes.
4. Let it soak for about 15 minutes.
5. Bake in the preheated oven for about 45 minutes or until the top is golden and set. "Bon appétit!"

Bulgur Wheat Salad

PREPARATION TIME
5'

COOK TIME
25'

SERVING
4

NUTRITION

Calories: 359
Fat: 15.5g
Carbs: 48.1g
Protein: 10.1g

INGREDIENTS

1 cup bulgur wheat
1 (½) cups vegetable broth
1 teaspoon sea salt
1 teaspoon fresh ginger, minced
4 tablespoons olive oil
1 onion, chopped
8 ounces canned garbanzo beans, drained
2 large roasted peppers, sliced
2 tablespoons fresh parsley, roughly chopped

DIRECTIONS

1. In a deep saucepan, bring the bulgur wheat and vegetable broth to a simmer; let it cook, covered, for 12 to 13 minutes.
2. Let it stand for about 10 minutes and fluff with a fork.
3. Add the remaining ingredients to the cooked bulgur wheat; serve at room temperature or well-chilled. "Bon appétit!"

Rye Porridge with Blueberry Topping

PREPARATION TIME
5'

COOK TIME
15'

SERVING
3

NUTRITION

Calories: 359
Fat: 11g
Carbs: 56.1g
Protein: 12.1g

INGREDIENTS

1 cup rye flakes
1 cup water
1 cup coconut milk
1 cup fresh blueberries
1 tablespoon coconut oil
6 dates, pitted

DIRECTIONS

1. Add the rye flakes, water and coconut milk to a deep saucepan; bring to a boil over medium-high. Turn the heat to a simmer and let it cook for 5 to 6 minutes.
2. In a blender or food processor, puree the blueberries with coconut oil and dates.
3. Ladle into three bowls and garnish with the blueberry topping. "Bon appétit!"

Coconut Sorghum Porridge

PREPARATION TIME
5'

COOK TIME
15'

SERVING
2

NUTRITION

Calories: 289
Fat: 5.1g
Carbs: 57.8g
Protein: 7.3g

INGREDIENTS

1/2 cup sorghum
1 cup water
1/2 cup coconut milk
1/4 teaspoon grated nutmeg
1/4 teaspoon ground cloves
1/2 teaspoon ground cinnamon
Kosher salt to taste
2 tablespoons agave syrup
2 tablespoons coconut flakes

DIRECTIONS

1. Place the sorghum, water, milk, nutmeg, cloves, cinnamon and kosher salt in a saucepan; simmer gently for about 15 minutes.
2. Spoon the porridge into serving bowls. Top with agave syrup and coconut flakes. "Bon appétit!"

Dad's Aromatic Rice

INGREDIENTS

3 tablespoons olive oil
1 teaspoon garlic, minced
1 teaspoon dried oregano
1 teaspoon dried rosemary
1 bay leaf
1 (½) cups white rice
½ cup vegetable broth
Sea salt and cayenne pepper to taste

PREPARATION TIME
5'

COOK TIME
20'

SERVING
4

NUTRITION

Calories: 384
Fat: 11.4g
Carbs: 60.4g
Protein: 8.3g

DIRECTIONS

1. In a saucepan, heat the olive oil over a moderately high flame. Add in the garlic, oregano, rosemary and bay leaf; sauté for about 1 minute or until aromatic.
2. Add in the rice and broth. Bring to a boil; immediately turn the heat to a gentle simmer.
3. Cook for about 15 minutes or until all the liquid has been absorbed. Fluff the rice with a fork, season with salt and pepper and serve immediately.

Everyday Savory Grits

PREPARATION TIME
5'

COOK TIME
35'

SERVING
4

NUTRITION

Calories: 238
Fat: 6.5g
Carbs: 38.7g
Protein: 3.7g

INGREDIENTS

2 tablespoons vegan butter
1 sweet onion, chopped
1 teaspoon garlic, minced
4 cups water
1 cup stone-ground grits
Sea salt and cayenne pepper to taste

DIRECTIONS

1. In a saucepan, melt the vegan butter over medium-high heat. Once hot, cook the onion for about 3 minutes or until tender.
2. Add in the garlic and continue to sauté for 30 seconds more or until aromatic, reserve.
3. Bring the water to a boil over moderately high heat. Stir in the grits, salt and pepper. Turn the heat to a simmer, cover and continue to cook, for about 30 minutes or until cooked through.
4. Stir in the sautéed mixture and serve warm. "Bon appétit!"

Greek-Style Barley Salad

PREPARATION TIME 5'

COOK TIME 35'

SERVING 4

NUTRITION

Calories: 378
Fat: 15.6g
Carbs: 50g
Protein: 10.7g

INGREDIENTS

1 cup pearl barley
2 (¾) cups vegetable broth
2 tablespoons apple cider vinegar
4 tablespoons Extra-virgin olive oil
2 bell peppers, seeded and diced
1 shallot, chopped
2 ounces sun-dried tomatoes in oil, chopped
1 green olive, pitted and sliced
2 tablespoons fresh cilantro, roughly chopped

DIRECTIONS

1. Bring the barley and broth to a boil over medium-high heat; now, turn the heat to a simmer.
2. Continue to simmer for about 30 minutes until all the liquid has been absorbed; fluff with a fork.
3. Toss the barley with vinegar, olive oil, peppers, shallots, sun-dried tomatoes and olive; toss to combine well.
4. Garnish with fresh cilantro and serve at room temperature or well-chilled. Enjoy!

Easy Sweet Maize Meal Porridge

PREPARATION TIME
5'

COOK TIME
15'

SERVING
2

NUTRITION

Calories: 278
Fat: 12.7g
Carbs: 37.2g
Protein: 3g

INGREDIENTS

2 cups water
1/2 cup maize meal
1/4 teaspoon ground allspice
1/4 teaspoon salt
2 tablespoons brown sugar
2 tablespoons almond butter

DIRECTIONS

1. In a saucepan, bring the water to a boil, then gradually add in the maize meal and turn the heat to a simmer.
2. Add in the ground allspice and salt. Let it cook for 10 minutes.
3. Add in the brown sugar and almond butter and gently stir to combine. "Bon appétit!"

Mom's Millet Muffins

PREPARATION TIME
5'

COOK TIME
20'

SERVING
8

NUTRITION

Calories: 367
Fat: 15.9g
Carbs: 53.7g
Protein: 6.5g

INGREDIENTS

2 cups whole-wheat flour
1/2 cup millet
2 teaspoons baking powder
1/2 teaspoon salt
1 cup coconut milk
1/2 cup coconut oil, melted
1/2 cup agave nectar
1/2 teaspoon ground cinnamon
1/4 teaspoon ground cloves
A pinch of grated nutmeg
1/2 cup dried apricots, chopped

DIRECTIONS

1. Begin by preheating your oven to 400°F. Lightly oil a muffin tin with nonstick oil.
2. In a mixing bowl, mix all dry ingredients. In a separate bowl, mix the wet ingredients. Stir the milk mixture into the flour mixture; mix just until evenly moist and do not over-mix your batter.
3. Fold in the apricots and scrape the batter into the prepared muffin cups.
4. Bake the muffins in the preheated oven for about 15 minutes, or until a tester inserted in the center of your muffin comes out dry and clean.
5. Let it stand for 10 minutes on a wire rack before unfolding and serving. Enjoy!

Ginger Brown Rice

INGREDIENTS

½ cup brown rice, rinsed
2 tablespoons olive oil
1 teaspoon garlic, minced
1 (1-inch) piece ginger, peeled and minced
½ teaspoon cumin seeds
Sea salt and ground black pepper to taste

PREPARATION TIME
5'

COOK TIME
30'

SERVING
4

NUTRITION

Calories: 318
Fat: 8.8g
Carbs: 53.4g
Protein: 5.6g

DIRECTIONS

1. Place the brown rice in a saucepan and cover it with cold water by 2-inches. Bring to a boil.
2. Turn the heat to a simmer and continue to cook for about 30 minutes or until tender.
3. In a sauté pan, heat the olive oil over medium-high heat. Once hot, cook the garlic, ginger and cumin seeds until aromatic.
4. Stir the garlic/ginger mixture into the hot rice; season with salt and pepper and serve immediately. "Bon appétit!"

Sweet Oatmeal "Grits"

PREPARATION TIME
5'

COOK TIME
20'

SERVING
4

NUTRITION

Calories: 380
Fat: 11.1g
Carbs: 59g
Protein: 14.4g

INGREDIENTS

½ cup steel-cut oats, soaked overnight
1 cup almond milk
4 cups water
A pinch of grated nutmeg
A pinch of ground cloves
A pinch of sea salt
4 tablespoons almonds, slivered
6 dates, pitted and chopped
6 prunes, chopped

DIRECTIONS

1. In a deep saucepan, bring the steel-cut oats, almond milk and water to a boil.
2. Add in the nutmeg, cloves and salt. Immediately turn the heat to a simmer, cover and continue to cook for about 15 minutes or until they've softened.
3. Then, spoon the grits into four serving bowls; top them with the almonds, dates and prunes. "Bon appétit!"

Freekeh Bowl with Dried Figs

PREPARATION TIME
5'

COOK TIME
35'

SERVING
2

NUTRITION

Calories: 458
Fat: 6.8g
Carbs: 90g
Protein: 12.4g

INGREDIENTS

1/2 cup freekeh, soaked for 30 minutes, drained
1/3 cup almond milk
1/4 teaspoon sea salt
1/4 teaspoon ground cloves
1/4 teaspoon ground cinnamon
4 tablespoons agave syrup
2 ounces dried figs, chopped

DIRECTIONS

1. Place the freekeh, milk, sea salt, ground cloves and cinnamon in a saucepan. Bring to a boil over medium-high heat.
2. Immediately turn the heat to a simmer for 30 to 35 minutes, stirring occasionally to promote even cooking.
3. Stir in the agave syrup and figs. Ladle the porridge into individual bowls and serve. "Bon appétit!"

Cornmeal Porridge with Maple Syrup

PREPARATION TIME
5'

COOK TIME
20'

SERVING
4

NUTRITION

Calories: 328
Fat: 4.8g
Carbs: 63.4g
Protein: 6.6g

INGREDIENTS

2 cups water
2 cups almond milk
1 cinnamon stick
1 vanilla bean
1 cup yellow cornmeal
1/2 cup maple syrup

DIRECTIONS

1. In a saucepan, bring the water and almond milk to a boil. Add in the cinnamon stick and vanilla bean.
2. Gradually add in the cornmeal, stirring continuously; turn the heat to a simmer. Let it simmer for about 15 minutes.
3. Drizzle the maple syrup over the porridge and serve warm. Enjoy!

CHAPTER 12
SMOOTHIES AND BEVERAGES RECIPES

Max Power Smoothie

INGREDIENTS

1 banana
¼ cup rolled oats, or 1 scoop plant protein powder
1 tablespoon flaxseed, or chia seeds
1 cup raspberries, or other berries
1 cup chopped mango (frozen or fresh)
½ cup non-dairy milk (optional)
1 cup water

DIRECTIONS

1. Purée everything in a blender until smooth, adding more water (or non-dairy milk) if needed.
2. Add none, some, or all the bonus boosters, as desired. Purée until blended.

PREPARATION TIME
5'

COOK TIME
0'

SERVING
4

NUTRITION

Calories: 550
Fat: 9g
Carbs: 116g
Fiber: 29g
Protein: 13g

CHAI CHIA SMOOTHIE

PREPARATION TIME
5'

COOK TIME
0'

SERVING
3

NUTRITION

Calories: 477
Fat: 29g
Carbs: 57g
Fiber: 14g
Protein: 8g

INGREDIENTS

1 banana
½ cup coconut milk
1 cup water
1 cup alfalfa sprouts (optional)
1 to 2 soft Medjool dates, pitted
1 tablespoon chia seeds, or ground flax or hemp hearts
¼ teaspoon ground cinnamon
A pinch of ground cardamom
1 tablespoon grated fresh ginger, or ¼ teaspoon ground ginger

DIRECTIONS

1. Purée everything in a blender until smooth, adding more water (or coconut milk) if needed.

Trope-Kale Breeze

PREPARATION TIME
5'

COOK TIME
0'

SERVING
4

NUTRITION

Calories: 566
Fat: 36g
Carbs: 66g
Fiber: 12g
Protein: 8g

INGREDIENTS

1 cup chopped pineapple (frozen or fresh)
1 cup chopped mango (frozen or fresh)
½ to 1 cup kale, chopped
½ avocado
½ cup coconut milk
1 cup water (or coconut water)
1 teaspoon matcha green tea powder (optional)

DIRECTIONS

1. Purée everything in a blender until smooth, add more water (or coconut milk) if needed.

HYDRATION STATION

PREPARATION TIME
5'

COOK TIME
0'

SERVING
4

NUTRITION

Calories: 320
Fat: 3g
Carbs: 76g
Fiber: 13g
Protein: 6g

INGREDIENTS

1 banana
1 orange, peeled and sectioned, or 1 cup pure orange juice
1 cup strawberries (frozen or fresh)
1 cup chopped cucumber
½ cup coconut water
1 cup water
½ cup ice

DIRECTIONS

1. Purée everything in a blender until smooth, adding more water if needed.
2. Add bonus boosters, as desired, and purée until blended.

Mango Madness

INGREDIENTS

1 banana
1 cup chopped mango (frozen or fresh)
1 cup chopped peach (frozen or fresh)
1 cup strawberries
1 carrot, peeled and chopped (optional)
1 cup water

PREPARATION TIME
5'

COOK TIME
0'

SERVING
4

NUTRITION

Calories: 376
Fat: 2g
Carbs: 95g
Fiber: 14g
Protein: 5g

DIRECTIONS

1. Purée everything in a blender until smooth, adding more water if needed.

Chocolate PB Smoothie

INGREDIENTS

1 banana
¼ cup rolled oats, or 1 scoop plant protein powder
1 tablespoon flaxseed or chia seeds
1 tablespoon unsweetened cocoa powder
1 tablespoon peanut butter, or almond or sunflower seed butter
1 tablespoon maple syrup (optional)
1 cup alfalfa sprouts or spinach, chopped (optional)
½ cup non-dairy milk (optional)
1 cup water

PREPARATION TIME
5'

COOK TIME
0'

SERVING
4

DIRECTIONS

1. Purée everything in a blender until smooth, add more water (or non-dairy milk) if needed.
2. Add bonus boosters, as desired, and purée until blended.

NUTRITION

Calories: 474
Fat: 16g
Carbs: 79g
Fiber: 18g
Protein: 13g

Pink Panther Smoothie

PREPARATION TIME
5'

COOK TIME
0'

SERVING
3

NUTRITION

Calories: 459
Fat: 30g
Carbs: 52g
Fiber: 19g
Protein: 8g

INGREDIENTS

1 cup strawberries
1 cup chopped melon (any kind)
1 cup cranberries or raspberries
1 tablespoon chia seeds
½ cup coconut milk or other non-dairy milk
1 cup water

DIRECTIONS

1. Purée everything in a blender until smooth, add more water (or coconut milk) if needed.
2. Add bonus boosters, as desired, and purée until blended.

Banana Nut Smoothie

INGREDIENTS

1 banana
1 tablespoon almond butter, or sunflower seed butter
¼ teaspoon ground cinnamon
A pinch of ground nutmeg
1 to 2 tablespoons dates, or maple syrup
1 tablespoon ground flaxseed, or chia or hemp hearts
½ cup non-dairy milk (optional)
1 cup water

DIRECTIONS

1. Purée everything in a blender until smooth, add more water (or non-dairy milk) if needed.

PREPARATION TIME
5'

COOK TIME
0'

SERVING
3

NUTRITION

Calories: 343
Fat: 14g
Carbs: 55g
Fiber: 8g
Protein: 6g

Light Ginger Tea

PREPARATION TIME
5'

COOK TIME
10'

SERVING
2

INGREDIENTS

1 small ginger knob, sliced into four 1-inch chunks
4 cups water
Juice of 1 large lemon
Maple syrup to taste

DIRECTIONS

1. Add the ginger knob and water in a saucepan, then simmer over medium heat for 10 to 15 minutes.
2. Turn off the heat, then mix in the lemon juice. Strain the liquid to remove the ginger, then fold in the maple syrup and serve.

NUTRITION

Calories: 32
Fat: 0.1g
Carbs: 8.6g
Fiber: 0.1g
Protein: 0.1g

Kale Smoothie

PREPARATION TIME
5'

COOK TIME
0'

SERVING
2

NUTRITION

Calories: 663
Fat: 10g
Carbs: 142.5g
Fiber: 19g
Protein: 17.4g

INGREDIENTS

2 cups chopped kale leaves
1 banana, peeled
1 cup frozen strawberries
1 cup unsweetened almond milk
4 Medjool dates, pitted and chopped

DIRECTIONS

1. Put all the ingredients in a food processor, then blitz until glossy and smooth.
2. Serve immediately or chill in the refrigerator for 1 hour before serving.

Hot Tropical Smoothie

INGREDIENTS

1 cup frozen mango chunks
1 cup frozen pineapple chunks
1 small tangerine, peeled and pitted
4 cups spinach leaves
1 cup coconut water
¼ teaspoon cayenne pepper, optional

PREPARATION TIME
5'

COOK TIME
0

SERVING
4

NUTRITION

Calories: 283
Fat: 1.9g
Carbs: 67.9g
Fiber: 10.4g
Protein: 6.4g

DIRECTIONS

1. Add all the ingredients to a food processor, then blitz until the mixture is smooth and combined well.
2. Serve immediately or chill in the refrigerator for 1 hour before serving.

Berry Smoothie

INGREDIENTS

1 cup berry mix (strawberries, blueberries and cranberries)
4 Medjool dates, pitted and chopped
1 ½ cups unsweetened almond milk, plus more as needed

PREPARATION TIME
5'

COOK TIME
0'

SERVING
4

DIRECTIONS

1. Add all the ingredients to a blender, then process until the mixture is smooth and well mixed.
2. Serve immediately or chill in the refrigerator for 1 hour before serving.

NUTRITION

Calories: 473
Fat: 4g
Carbs: 103.7g
Fiber: 9.7g
Protein: 14.8g

Cranberry and Banana Smoothie

INGREDIENTS

1 cup frozen cranberries
1 large banana, peeled
4 Medjool dates, pitted and chopped
1 ½ cups unsweetened almond milk

PREPARATION TIME
5'

COOK TIME
0'

SERVING
4

DIRECTIONS

1. Add all the ingredients to a food processor, then process until the mixture is glossy and well mixed.
2. Serve immediately or chill in the refrigerator for 1 hour before serving.

NUTRITION

Calories: 616
Fat: 8g
Carbs: 132.8g
Fiber: 14.6g
Protein: 15.7g

Pumpkin Smoothie

INGREDIENTS

½ cup pumpkin purée
4 Medjool dates, pitted and chopped
1 cup unsweetened almond milk
¼ teaspoon vanilla extract
¼ teaspoon ground cinnamon
½ cup ice
A pinch of ground nutmeg

PREPARATION TIME
5′

COOK TIME
0′

SERVING
2

DIRECTIONS

1. Add all the ingredients to a blender, then process until the mixture is glossy and well mixed.
2. Serve immediately.

NUTRITION

Calories: 417
Fat: 3g
Carbs: 94.9g
Fiber: 10.4g
Protein: 11.4g

Super Smoothie

PREPARATION TIME
5'

COOK TIME
0'

SERVING
4

NUTRITION

Calories: 550
Fat: 39g
Carbs: 31g
Fiber: 15g
Protein: 13g

INGREDIENTS

1 banana, peeled
1 cup chopped mango
1 cup raspberries
¼ cup rolled oats
1 carrot, peeled
1 cup chopped fresh kale
2 tablespoons chopped fresh parsley
1 tablespoon flaxseeds
1 tablespoon grated fresh ginger
½ cup unsweetened soy milk
1 cup water

DIRECTIONS

1. Put all the ingredients in a food processor, then blitz until glossy and smooth.
2. Serve immediately or chill in the refrigerator for 1 hour before serving.

Kiwi and Strawberry Smoothie

PREPARATION TIME
5'

COOK TIME
0'

SERVING
3

NUTRITION

Calories: 562
Fat: 28.6g
Carbs: 63.6g
Fiber: 15.1g
Protein: 23.3g

INGREDIENTS

1 kiwi, peeled
5 medium strawberries
½ frozen banana
1 cup unsweetened almond milk
2 tablespoons hemp seeds
2 tablespoons peanut butter
1 to 2 teaspoons maple syrup
½ cup spinach leaves
Handful broccoli sprouts

DIRECTIONS

1. Put all the ingredients in a food processor, then blitz until creamy and smooth.
2. Serve immediately or chill in the refrigerator for 1 hour before serving.

Banana and Chai Chia Smoothie

PREPARATION TIME
5'

COOK TIME
0'

SERVING
3

NUTRITION

Calories: 477
Fat: 41g
Carbs: 31g
Fiber: 14g
Protein: 8g

INGREDIENTS

1 banana
1 cup alfalfa sprouts
1 tablespoon chia seeds
½ cup unsweetened coconut milk
1 to 2 soft Medjool dates, pitted
¼ teaspoon ground cinnamon
1 tablespoon grated fresh ginger
1 cup water
A pinch of ground cardamom

DIRECTIONS

1. Add all the ingredients to a blender, then process until the mixture is smooth and creamy. Add water or coconut milk if necessary.
2. Serve immediately.

Chocolate and Peanut Butter Smoothie

PREPARATION TIME
5'

COOK TIME
0'

SERVING
4

NUTRITION

Calories: 474
Fat: 16g
Carbs: 27g
Fiber: 18g
Protein: 13g

INGREDIENTS

1 tablespoon unsweetened cocoa powder
1 tablespoon peanut butter
1 banana
1 teaspoon maca powder
½ cup unsweetened soy milk
¼ cup rolled oats
1 tablespoon flaxseeds
1 tablespoon maple syrup
1 cup water

DIRECTIONS

1. Add all the ingredients to a blender, then process until the mixture is smooth and creamy. Add water or soy milk if necessary.
2. Serve immediately.

Golden Milk

PREPARATION TIME
5'

COOK TIME
0'

SERVING
4

NUTRITION

Calories: 577
Fat: 57.3g
Carbs: 19.7g
Fiber: 6.1g
Protein: 5.7g

INGREDIENTS

¼ teaspoon ground cinnamon
½ teaspoon ground turmeric
½ teaspoon grated fresh ginger
1 teaspoon maple syrup
1 cup unsweetened coconut milk
Ground black pepper to taste
2 tablespoons water

DIRECTIONS

1. Combine all the ingredients in a saucepan. Stir to mix well.
2. Heat over medium heat for 5 minutes. Keep stirring during the heating.
3. Allow to cool for 5 minutes, then pour the mixture into a blender. Pulse until creamy and smooth. Serve immediately.

Mango Agua Fresca

PREPARATION TIME
5'

COOK TIME
0'

SERVING
2

NUTRITION

Calories: 230
Fat: 1.3g
Carbs: 57.7g
Fiber: 5.4g
Protein: 2.8g

INGREDIENTS

2 fresh mangoes, diced
1 ½ cups water
1 teaspoon fresh lime juice
Maple syrup to taste
2 cups ice
2 slices fresh lime for garnish
2 fresh mint sprigs for garnish

DIRECTIONS

1. Put the mangoes, lime juice, maple syrup and water into a blender. Process until creamy and smooth.
2. Divide the beverage into two glasses, then garnish each glass with ice, lime slice and mint sprig before serving.

Chapter 13
Snacks Recipes

Cinnamon and Hemp Seed Coffee Shake

PREPARATION TIME
5'

COOK TIME
0'

SERVING
1

NUTRITION

Calories: 410
Fat: 19.5g
Protein: 4.9g
Carbs: 60.8g
Fiber: 6.8g

INGREDIENTS

1 1/2 frozen bananas, sliced into coins
1/8 teaspoon ground cinnamon
2 tablespoons hemp seeds
1 tablespoon maple syrup
1/4 teaspoon vanilla extract, unsweetened
1 cup regular coffee, cooled
1/4 cup almond milk, unsweetened
1/2 cup of ice cubes

DIRECTIONS

1. Pour milk into a blender, add vanilla, cinnamon and hemp seeds and then pulse until smooth.
2. Add banana, pour in the coffee, and then pulse until smooth.
3. Add ice, blend until well combined, blend in maple syrup and then serve.

Green Smoothie

PREPARATION TIME
5'

COOK TIME
0'

SERVING
1

NUTRITION

Calories: 204
Fat: 1.1g
Protein: 6.5g
Carbs: 48g
Fiber: 8.3g

INGREDIENTS

½ cup strawberries, frozen
4 leaves of kale
¼ of a medium banana
2 Medjool dates, pitted
1 tablespoon flax seed
¼ cup pumpkin seeds, hulled
1 cup of water

DIRECTIONS

1. Place all the ingredients in the jar of a food processor or blender, and then cover it with the lid.
2. Pulse until smooth and then serve.

Strawberry and Banana Smoothie

PREPARATION TIME
5'

COOK TIME
0'

SERVING
1

NUTRITION

Calories: 114
Fat: 2.1g
Protein: 3.7g
Carbs: 22.3g
Fiber: 3.8g

INGREDIENTS

1 cup sliced banana, frozen
2 tablespoons chia seeds
2 cups strawberries, frozen
2 teaspoons honey
¼ teaspoon vanilla extract, unsweetened
6 ounces coconut yogurt
1 cup almond milk, unsweetened

DIRECTIONS

1. Place all the ingredients in the jar of a food processor or blender, and then cover it with the lid.
2. Pulse until smooth and then serve.

Orange Smoothie

PREPARATION TIME
5'

COOK TIME
0'

SERVING
1

NUTRITION

Calories: 198.7
Fat: 1.2g
Protein: 6.1g
Carbs: 34.3g
Fiber: 0g

INGREDIENTS

1 cup slices of oranges
½ teaspoon grated ginger
1 cup of mango pieces
1 cup of coconut water
1 cup chopped strawberries
1 cup crushed ice

DIRECTIONS

1. Place all the ingredients in the jar of a food processor or blender, and then cover it with the lid.
2. Pulse until smooth and then serve.

Pumpkin Chai Smoothie

PREPARATION TIME
5'

COOK TIME
0'

SERVING
1

NUTRITION

Calories: 157.5
Fat: 3.8g
Protein: 3g
Carbs: 32.3g
Fiber: 4.5g

INGREDIENTS

1 cup cooked pumpkin
¼ cup pecans
1 frozen banana
¼ teaspoon ground cinnamon
¼ teaspoon cardamom
¼ teaspoon ground nutmeg
2 teaspoons maple syrup
1 cup of water, cold
½ cup of ice cubes

DIRECTIONS

1. Place pecans in a small bowl, cover with water, and then let them soak for 10 minutes.
2. Drain the pecans, add them into a blender, and then add the remaining ingredients.
3. Pulse for 1 minute until smooth and then serve.

Banana Shake

PREPARATION TIME
5'

COOK TIME
0'

SERVING
1

NUTRITION

Calories: 301
Fat: 9.3g
Protein: 6.8g
Carbs: 49g
Fiber: 1.9g

INGREDIENTS

3 medium frozen bananas
1 tablespoon cocoa powder, unsweetened
1 teaspoon shredded coconut
1 tablespoon maple syrup
1 tablespoon peanut butter
1 teaspoon vanilla extract, unsweetened
2 cups of coconut water
1 cup of ice cubes

DIRECTIONS

1. Add banana in a food processor, add maple syrup and vanilla, pour in water and then add ice.
2. Pulse until smooth and then pour half of the smoothie into a glass.
3. Add butter and cocoa powder into the blender, pulse until smooth, and then add to the smoothie glass.
4. Sprinkle coconut over the smoothie and then serve.

Green Honeydew Smoothie

PREPARATION TIME
5'

COOK TIME
15'

SERVING
4

INGREDIENTS

1 large banana
6 large leaves of basil
½ cup frozen pineapple
1 teaspoon lime juice
1 cup pieces of Honeydew melon
1 teaspoon green tea matcha powder
¼ cup almond milk, unsweetened

DIRECTIONS

1. Place all the ingredients in the jar of a food processor or blender, and then cover it with the lid.
2. Pulse until smooth and then serve.

NUTRITION

Calories: 223.5
Fat: 2.7g
Protein: 20.1g
Carbs: 32.7g
Fiber: 5.2g

Summer Salsa

PREPARATION TIME
5'

COOK TIME
15'

SERVING
8

NUTRITION

Calories: 51
Fat: 0.1g
Protein: 1.7g
Carbs: 11.4g
Fiber: 3.1g

INGREDIENTS

1 cup cherry tomatoes chopped
1/4 cup chopped cilantro
2 tablespoons chopped red onion
1 teaspoon minced garlic
1 small jalapeno, seeded, chopped
1/2 of a lime, juiced
1/8 teaspoon salt
1 tablespoon olive oil

DIRECTIONS

1. Place all the ingredients in the jar of a food processor or blender except for cilantro, and then cover with its lid.
2. Pulse until smooth and then pulse in cilantro until evenly mixed.
3. Tip the salsa into a bowl and then serve with vegetable sticks.

Red Salsa

INGREDIENTS

4 Roma tomatoes, halved
¼ cup chopped cilantro
1 jalapeno pepper, seeded, halved
½ of a medium white onion, peeled, cut into quarters
3 cloves of garlic, peeled
½ teaspoon salt
1 tablespoon brown sugar
1 teaspoon apple cider vinegar

PREPARATION TIME
35′

COOK TIME
15′

SERVING
8

NUTRITION

Calories: 240
Fat: 0g
Protein: 0g
Carbs: 48g
Fiber: 16g

DIRECTIONS

1. Switch on the oven, then set it to 425°F and let it preheat.
2. Meanwhile, take a baking sheet, line it with foil and then spread tomato, jalapeno pepper, onion and garlic.
3. Bake the vegetables for 15 minutes until vegetables have cooked and begin to brown, and then let the vegetables cool for 3 minutes.
4. Transfer the roasted vegetables into a blender, add the remaining ingredients and then pulse until smooth.
5. Tip the salsa into a medium bowl and then chill it for 30 minutes before serving with vegetable sticks.

Pinto Bean Dip

INGREDIENTS

15 ounces canned pinto beans
1 jalapeno pepper
2 teaspoons ground cumin
3 tablespoons nutritional yeast
1/3 cup basil salsa

PREPARATION TIME
5'

COOK TIME
0'

SERVING
4

DIRECTIONS

1. Place all the ingredients in a food processor, cover with the lid and then pulse until smooth.
2. Tip the dip in a bowl and then serve with vegetable slices.

NUTRITION

Calories: 360
Fat: 0g
Protein: 24g
Carbs: 72g
Fiber: 24g

Smoky Red Pepper Hummus

PREPARATION TIME
5'

COOK TIME
0'

SERVING
4

NUTRITION

Calories: 489
Fat: 30g
Protein: 9g
Carbs: 15g
Fiber: 6g

INGREDIENTS

1/4 cup roasted red peppers
1 cup cooked chickpeas
1/8 teaspoon garlic powder
1/2 teaspoon salt
1/8 teaspoon ground black pepper
1/4 teaspoon ground cumin
1/4 teaspoon red chili powder
1 tablespoon tahini
2 tablespoons water

DIRECTIONS

1. Place all the ingredients in the jar of the food processor and then pulse until smooth.
2. Tip the hummus in a bowl and then serve with vegetable slices.

Spinach Dip

PREPARATION TIME
20'

COOK TIME
5'

SERVING
8

NUTRITION

Calories: 134.6
Fat: 8.6g
Protein: 10g
Carbs: 6.3g
Fiber: 1.4g

INGREDIENTS

¾ cup cashews
3.5 ounces soft tofu
6 ounces of spinach leaves
1 medium white onion, peeled, diced
2 teaspoons minced garlic
½ teaspoon salt
3 tablespoons olive oil

DIRECTIONS

1. Place cashews in a bowl, cover with hot water, and then let them soak for 15 minutes.
2. After 15 minutes, drain the cashews and then set them aside until required.
3. Take a medium skillet pan, add oil to it and then place the pan over medium heat.
4. Add onion, cook for 3 to 5 minutes until tender, stir in garlic and then continue cooking for 30 seconds until fragrant.
5. Spoon the onion mixture into a blender, add the remaining ingredients and then pulse until smooth.
6. Tip the dip into a bowl and then serve with chips.

Tomatillo Salsa

PREPARATION TIME
5'

COOK TIME
20'

SERVING
8

NUTRITION

Calories: 317.4
Fat: 0g
Protein: 16g
Carbs: 64g
Fiber: 16g

INGREDIENTS

5 medium tomatillos, chopped
3 cloves of garlic, peeled, chopped
3 Roma tomatoes, chopped
1 jalapeno, chopped
½ of a medium red onion, peeled, chopped
1 Anaheim chili
2 teaspoons salt
1 teaspoon ground cumin
1 lime, juiced
¼ cup cilantro leaves
¾ cup of water

DIRECTIONS

1. Take a medium pot, place it over medium heat, pour in water and then add onion, garlic, tomatoes, tomatillo, jalapeno and Anaheim chili.
2. Sauté the vegetables for 15 minutes, remove the pot from heat, add cilantro, cumin and lime juice and then stir in salt.
3. Remove the pot from heat and then pulse by using an immersion blender until smooth.
4. Serve the salsa with chips.

Arugula Pesto Couscous

PREPARATION TIME
10'

COOK TIME
20'

SERVING
4

NUTRITION

Calories: 73
Fat: 4g
Protein: 2g
Carbs: 8g
Fiber: 2g

INGREDIENTS

8 ounces Israeli couscous
3 large tomatoes, chopped
3 cups arugula leaves
½ cup parsley leaves
6 cloves of garlic, peeled
½ cup walnuts
¾ teaspoon salt
1 cup and 1 tablespoon olive oil
2 cups vegetable broth

DIRECTIONS

1. Take a medium saucepan, place it over medium-high heat, add 1 tablespoon oil and then let it heat.
2. Add couscous, stir until mixed, and then cook for 4 minutes until fragrant and toasted.
3. Pour in the broth, stir until mixed, bring it to a boil, switch heat to medium level and then simmer for 12 minutes until the couscous has been absorbed all the liquid and turn tender.
4. When done, remove the pan from heat, fluff it with a fork, and then set it aside until required.
5. While couscous cooks, prepare the pesto and for this, place walnuts in a blender, add garlic and then pulse until nuts have broken.
6. Add arugula, parsley and salt, pulse until well combined, and then blend in oil until smooth.
7. Transfer couscous to a salad bowl, add tomatoes and the prepared pesto, and then toss until mixed.
8. Serve straight away.

Oatmeal and Raisin Balls

PREPARATION TIME
42'

COOK TIME
0'

SERVING
4

NUTRITION

Calories: 135
Fat: 6g
Protein: 8g
Carbs: 13g
Fiber: 4g

INGREDIENTS

1 cup rolled oats
¼ cup raisins
½ cup peanut butter

DIRECTIONS

1. Place oats in a large bowl, add raisins and peanut butter, and then stir until well combined.
2. Shape the mixture into twelve balls, 1 tablespoon of mixture per ball, and then arrange the balls on a baking sheet.
3. Place the baking sheet into the freezer for 30 minutes until firm and then serve.

NACHO CHEESE

PREPARATION TIME
10'

COOK TIME
15'

SERVING
4

NUTRITION

Calories: 611.7
Fat: 17.2g
Protein: 32.1g
Carbs: 62.1g
Fiber: 12.1g

INGREDIENTS

1 cup chopped carrots
½ teaspoon onion powder
2 cups peeled and chopped potatoes
½ teaspoon garlic powder
1 teaspoon salt
½ cup nutritional yeast
1 tablespoon lemon juice
¼ cup of salsa
½ cup of water

DIRECTIONS

1. Take a medium pot, place carrots and potato in it, cover with water and then place the pot over medium-high heat.
2. Boil the vegetables for 10 minutes, drain them and then transfer them into a blender.
3. Add the remaining ingredients and then pulse until smooth.
4. Tip the cheese into a bowl and then serve with vegetable slices.

Pico de Gallo

INGREDIENTS

1/2 of a medium red onion, peeled, chopped
2 cups diced tomato
1/2 cup chopped cilantro
1 jalapeno pepper, minced
1/8 teaspoon salt
1/4 teaspoon ground black pepper
1/2 of a lime, juiced
1 teaspoon olive oil

PREPARATION TIME
5'

COOK TIME
0'

SERVING
6

NUTRITION

Calories: 790
Fat: 6.4g
Protein: 25.6g
Carbs: 195.2g
Fiber: 35.2g

DIRECTIONS

1. Take a large bowl, place all the ingredients in it and then stir until well mixed.
2. Serve the Pico de Gallo with chips.

Beet Balls

PREPARATION TIME
10'

COOK TIME
0'

SERVING
6

NUTRITION

Calories: 114.2
Fat: 2.4g
Protein: 5g
Carbs: 19.6g
Fiber: 4.9g

INGREDIENTS

1/2 cup oats
1 medium beet, cooked
1/2 cup almond flour
1/3 cup shredded coconut and more for coating
3/4 cup Medjool dates, pitted
1 tablespoon cocoa powder
1/2 cup peanuts
1/4 cup chocolate chips, unsweetened

DIRECTIONS

1. Place cooked beet in a blender and then pulse until chopped into very small pieces.
2. Add the remaining ingredients and then pulse until the dough comes together.
3. Shape the dough into eighteen balls, coat them in some more coconut and then serve.

Cheesy Crackers

PREPARATION TIME
10'

COOK TIME
20'

SERVING
3

NUTRITION

Calories: 30
Fat: 1g
Protein: 1g
Carbs: 5g
Fiber: 0g

INGREDIENTS

1 ¾ cups almond meal
3 tablespoons nutritional yeast
½ teaspoon and a pinch of sea salt
2 tablespoons lemon juice
1 tablespoon melted coconut oil
1 tablespoon ground flaxseed
2 (½) tablespoons water

DIRECTIONS

1. Switch on the oven, then set it to 350°F and let it preheat.
2. Meanwhile, take a medium bowl, place flaxseed in it, stir in water and then let the mixture rest for 5 minutes until thickened.
3. Place almond meal in a medium bowl, add sea salt and yeast, and then stir until mixed.
4. Add lemon juice and coconut oil into the flaxseed mixture and then whisk until mixed.
5. Pour the flaxseed mixture into the almond meal mixture, and then stir until the dough comes together.
6. Place a piece of wax paper on a clean working space, place the dough on it, cover with another piece of wax paper, and then roll dough into a 1/8-inch thick crust.
7. Cut the dough into a square shape, sprinkle salt over the top and then bake for 15 to 20 minutes until done.
8. Serve straight away.

Tomato Soup

INGREDIENTS

56 ounces stewed tomatoes
¼ teaspoon salt
¼ teaspoon ground black pepper
1 medium red bell pepper, cored, diced
¼ teaspoon dried thyme
6 leaves of basil, chopped
¼ teaspoon dried oregano
1 teaspoon olive oil

PREPARATION TIME
10'

COOK TIME
10'

SERVING
2

DIRECTIONS

1. Take a medium pot, place it over medium heat, add oil and, when hot, add bell pepper and then cook for 4 minutes.
2. Add the remaining ingredients into the pot, stir until mixed, switch to medium-high heat and bring the mixture to simmer.
3. Remove pot from the heat and then puree the soup until smooth.
4. Taste to adjust seasoning, ladle soup into bowls and then serve.

NUTRITION

Calories: 170
Fat: 1.1g
Protein: 3.5g
Carbs: 36g
Fiber: 2.6g

Chapter 14
Desserts Recipes

Raspberry Muffins

PREPARATION TIME
10'

COOK TIME
25'

SERVING
12

NUTRITION

Calories: 109
Fat: 3.4g
Protein: 2.1g
Carbs: 17.6g
Fiber: 1g

INGREDIENTS

1/2 cup and 2 tablespoons whole-wheat flour
1 (1/2) cups raspberries, fresh and more for decorating
1 cup white whole-wheat flour
1/8 teaspoon salt
3/4 cup of coconut sugar
2 teaspoons baking powder
1 teaspoon apple cider vinegar
1 1/4 cups water
1/2 cup olive oil

DIRECTIONS

1. Switch on the oven, then set it to 400°F and let it preheat.
2. Meanwhile, take a large bowl, place both flours in it, add salt and baking powder and then stir until combined.
3. Take a medium bowl, add oil to it and then whisk in the sugar until dissolved.
4. Whisk in vinegar and water until blended, slowly stir in flour mixture until smooth batter comes together, and then fold in berries.
5. Take a 12-cups muffin pan, grease it with oil, fill evenly with the prepared mixture and then put a raspberry on top of each muffin.
6. Bake the muffins for 25 minutes until the top is golden brown and then serve.

Chocolate Chip Cake

PREPARATION TIME
10'

COOK TIME
50'

SERVING
10

NUTRITION

Calories: 218
Fat: 8g
Protein: 3.4g
Carbs: 32g
Fiber: 2g

INGREDIENTS

2 cups white whole-wheat flour
1/4 teaspoon baking soda
1/3 cup coconut sugar
2 teaspoons baking powder
1/2 teaspoon salt
1/2 cup chocolate chips, vegan
1 teaspoon vanilla extract, unsweetened
1 tablespoon applesauce
1 teaspoon apple cider vinegar
1/4 cup melted coconut oil
1/2 teaspoon almond extract, unsweetened
1 cup almond milk, unsweetened

DIRECTIONS

1. Switch on the oven, then set it to 360°F and let it preheat.
2. Meanwhile, take a 9 x 5-inches loaf pan, grease it with oil and then set aside until required.
3. Take a large bowl, add sugar to it, pour in oil, vanilla and almond extract, vinegar, applesauce and milk, and then whisk until well combined.
4. Take a large bowl, place flour in it, add salt, baking powder and soda, and then stir until mixed.
5. Stir the flour mixture into the milk mixture until smooth batter comes together and then fold in 1/3 cup of chocolate chips.
6. Spoon the batter into the loaf pan, scatter the remaining chocolate chips on top and then bake for 50 minutes.
7. When done, let the bread cool for 10 minutes and then cut it into slices.
8. Serve straight away.

Coffee Cake

PREPARATION TIME
10'

COOK TIME
45'

SERVING
9

NUTRITION

Calories: 259
Fat: 10g
Protein: 3g
Carbs: 37g
Fiber: 1g

INGREDIENTS

FOR THE CAKE:
1/3 cup coconut sugar
1 teaspoon vanilla extract, unsweetened
1/4 cup olive oil
1/8 teaspoon almond extract, unsweetened
1 3/4 cup white whole-wheat flour
2 teaspoons baking powder
1/2 teaspoon salt
1/4 teaspoon baking soda
1 teaspoon apple cider vinegar
1 tablespoon applesauce
1 cup almond milk, unsweetened

FOR THE STREUSEL BREAD:
1/2 cup white whole-wheat flour
2 teaspoons cinnamon
1/3 cup coconut sugar
1/2 teaspoon salt
2 tablespoons olive oil
1 tablespoon coconut butter

DIRECTIONS

1. Switch on the oven, then set it to 350°F and let it preheat.
2. Meanwhile, take a large bowl, pour in milk, add applesauce, vinegar, sugar, oil, vanilla and almond extract and then whisk until blended.
3. Take a medium bowl, place flour in it, add salt, baking powder and soda, and then stir until mixed.
4. Stir the flour mixture into the milk mixture until smooth batter comes together and then spoon the mixture into a loaf pan lined with parchment paper.
5. Prepare Streusel bread and for this, take a medium bowl, place flour in it and then add sugar, salt and cinnamon.
6. Stir until mixed, and then mix butter and oil with fingers until the crumble mixture comes together.
7. Spread the prepared Streusel on top of the batter of the cake, and then bake for 45 minutes until the top turn golden brown and the cake have thoroughly cooked.
8. When done, let the cake rest in its pan for 10 minutes, remove it to cool completely, and then cut it into slices.
9. Serve straight away.

Chocolate Marble Cake

PREPARATION TIME
15'

COOK TIME
50'

SERVING
8

NUTRITION

Calories: 299
Fat: 14g
Protein: 6g
Carbs: 39g
Fiber: 3g

INGREDIENTS

1 (1/2) cups white whole-wheat flour
1 tablespoon flaxseed meal
2 (1/2) tablespoons cocoa powder
1/4 teaspoon salt
4 tablespoons chopped walnuts
1 teaspoon baking powder
2/3 cup coconut sugar
1/4 teaspoon baking soda
1 teaspoon vanilla extract, unsweetened
3 tablespoons peanut butter
1/4 cup olive oil
1 cup almond milk, unsweetened

DIRECTIONS

1. Switch on the oven, then set it to 350°F and let it preheat.
2. Meanwhile, take a medium bowl, place flour in it, add salt, baking powder and soda in it and then stir until mixed.
3. Take a large bowl, pour in milk, add sugar, flaxseed meal, oil and vanilla, whisk until sugar has dissolved, and then whisk in flour mixture until smooth batter comes together.
4. Spoon half of the prepared batter in a medium bowl, add cocoa powder and then stir until combined.
5. Add peanut butter into the other bowl and then stir until combined.
6. Take a loaf pan, line it with a parchment sheet, spoon half of the chocolate batter in it, and then spread it evenly.
7. Layer the chocolate batter with half of the peanut butter batter, cover with the remaining chocolate batter and then layer with the remaining peanut butter batter.
8. Make swirls into the batter with a toothpick, smooth the top with a spatula, sprinkle walnuts on top, and then bake for 50 minutes until done.
9. When done, let the cake rest in its pan for 10 minutes, then remove it to cool completely and cut it into slices.
10. Serve straight away.

Chocolate Chip Cookies

PREPARATION TIME
10'

COOK TIME
10'

SERVING
11

NUTRITION

Calories: 141
Fat: 7g
Protein: 1g
Carbs: 17g
Fiber: 2g

INGREDIENTS

1 (¼) cups white whole-wheat flour
1 (½) tablespoons flax seeds
½ teaspoon baking soda
½ cup of coconut sugar
¼ teaspoon of sea salt
¼ cup powdered coconut sugar
1 teaspoon baking powder
2 teaspoons vanilla extract, unsweetened
4 (½) tablespoons water
½ cup of coconut oil
1 cup chocolate chips, vegan

DIRECTIONS

1. Take a large bowl, place flax seeds in it, stir in water and then let the mixture rest for 5 minutes until creamy.
2. Then add the remaining ingredients into the flax seed's mixture except for flour and chocolate chips, and then beat until light batter comes together.
3. Beat in flour, ¼ cup at a time, until smooth batter comes together, and then fold in chocolate chips.
4. Use an ice cream scoop to scoop the batter onto a baking sheet lined with parchment sheet with some distance between cookies, and then bake for 10 minutes until cookies turn golden brown.
5. When done, let the cookies cool on the baking sheet for 3 minutes and then cool completely on the wire rack for 5 minutes.
6. Serve straight away.

Lemon Cake

PREPARATION TIME
10'

COOK TIME
50'

SERVING
9

NUTRITION

Calories: 275
Fat: 12g
Protein: 3g
Carbs: 38g
Fiber: 1g

INGREDIENTS

- 1 (1/2) cups white whole-wheat flour
- 1 (1/2) teaspoons baking powder
- 2 tablespoons almond flour
- 1 lemon, zested
- 1/4 teaspoon baking soda
- 1/8 teaspoon turmeric powder
- 1/3 teaspoon salt
- 1/4 teaspoon vanilla extract, unsweetened
- 1/3 cup lemon juice
- 1/2 cup maple syrup
- 1/4 cup olive oil
- 1/4 cup of water

FOR THE FROSTING:
- 1 tablespoon lemon juice
- 1/8 teaspoon salt
- 1/4 cup maple syrup
- 2 tablespoons powdered sugar
- 6 ounces vegan cream cheese, softened

DIRECTIONS

1. Switch on the oven, then set it to 350°F and let it preheat.
2. Take a large bowl, pour in water, lemon juice and oil, add vanilla extract and maple syrup and whisk until blended.
3. Whisk in flour, ¼ cup at a time until smooth, and then whisk in almond flour, salt, turmeric, lemon zest, baking soda and powder until well combined.
4. Take a loaf pan, grease it with oil, spoon the prepared batter in it and then bake for 50 minutes.
5. Meanwhile, prepare the frosting and for this, take a small bowl, place all the ingredients in it, whisk until smooth and then let it chill until required.
6. When the cake has cooked, let it cool for 10 minutes in its pan and then let it cool completely on the wire rack.
7. Spread the prepared frosting on top of the cake, slice the cake and then serve.

Banana Muffins

PREPARATION TIME
10'

COOK TIME
30'

SERVING
12

NUTRITION

Calories: 240
Fat: 9.3g
Protein: 2.6g
Carbs: 35.4g
Fiber: 2g

INGREDIENTS

1 (½) cups mashed banana
1 (½) cups and 2 tablespoons white whole-wheat flour, divided
¼ cup of coconut sugar
¾ cup rolled oats, divided
1 teaspoon ginger powder
1 tablespoon ground cinnamon, divided
2 teaspoons baking powder
½ teaspoon salt
1 teaspoon baking soda
1 tablespoon vanilla extract, unsweetened
½ cup maple syrup
1 tablespoon rum
½ cup of coconut oil

DIRECTIONS

1. Switch on the oven, then set it to 350°F and let it preheat.
2. Meanwhile, take a medium bowl, place 1 (½) cups flour in it, add ½ cup oats, ginger, baking powder and soda, salt and 2 teaspoons cinnamon and then stir until mixed.
3. Place ¼ cup of coconut oil in a heatproof bowl, melt it in the microwave oven and then whisk in maple syrup until combined.
4. Add mashed banana along with rum and vanilla, stir until combined and then whisk this mixture into the flour mixture until the smooth batter comes together.
5. Take a separate medium bowl, place the remaining oats and flour in it, add cinnamon, coconut sugar and coconut oil, and then stir with a fork until a crumbly mixture comes together.
6. Take a 12-cups muffin pan, fill evenly with prepared batter, top with oats mixture and then bake for 30 minutes until firm and the top turn golden brown.
7. When done, let the muffins cool for 5 minutes in its pan and then cool the muffins completely before serving.

No-Bake Cookies

PREPARATION TIME
30'

COOK TIME
0'

SERVING
9

NUTRITION

Calories: 213
Fat: 14.8g
Protein: 4g
Carbs: 17.3g
Fiber: 2.1g

INGREDIENTS

1 cup rolled oats
1/4 cup of cocoa powder
1/8 teaspoon salt
1 teaspoon vanilla extract, unsweetened
1/4 cup and 2 tablespoons peanut butter, divided
6 tablespoons coconut oil, divided
1/4 cup and 1 tablespoon maple syrup, divided

DIRECTIONS

1. Take a small saucepan, place it over low heat, add 5 tablespoons of coconut oil and then let it melt.
2. Whisk in 2 tablespoons peanut butter, salt, 1 teaspoon vanilla extract and ¼ cup each of cocoa powder and maple syrup, and then whisk until well combined.
3. Remove the pan from heat, stir in oats and then spoon the mixture evenly into 9 cups of a muffin pan.
4. Wipe clean the pan, return it over low heat, add the remaining coconut oil, maple syrup and peanut butter, stir until combined and then cook for 2 minutes until thoroughly warmed.
5. Drizzle the peanut butter sauce over the oats mixture in the muffin pan and then let it freeze for 20 minutes or more until set.
6. Serve straight away.

Peanut Butter and Oats Bars

PREPARATION TIME
40'

COOK TIME
8'

SERVING
8

NUTRITION

Calories: 274
Fat: 17g
Protein: 10g
Carbs: 19g
Fiber: 3g

INGREDIENTS

1 cup rolled oats
1/8 teaspoon salt
1/4 cup chocolate chips, vegan
1/4 cup maple syrup
1 cup peanut butter

DIRECTIONS

1. Take a medium saucepan, place it over medium heat, add peanut butter, salt and maple syrup and then whisk until combined and thickened; this will take 5 minutes.
2. Remove pan from heat, place oats in a bowl, pour peanut butter mixture on it and then stir until well combined.
3. Take an 8 x 6-inch baking dish, line it with a parchment sheet, spoon the oats mixture in it and then spread evenly, pressing the mixture into the dish.
4. Sprinkle the chocolate chips on top, press them into the bar mixture and then let the mixture rest in the refrigerator for 30 minutes or more until set.
5. When ready to eat, cut the bar mixture into even size pieces and then serve.

BAKED APPLES

PREPARATION TIME
5'

COOK TIME
20'

SERVING
4

NUTRITION

Calories: 170
Fat: 3.8g
Protein: 0.5g
Carbs: 31g
Fiber: 5.5g

INGREDIENTS

6 medium apples, peeled, cut into chunks
1 teaspoon ground cinnamon
2 tablespoons melted coconut oil

DIRECTIONS

1. Switch on the oven, then set it to 350°F and let it preheat.
2. Take a medium baking dish and then spread apple pieces in it.
3. Take a small bowl, place coconut oil in it, stir in cinnamon, drizzle this mixture over apples and then toss until coated.
4. Place the baking dish into the oven and then bake for 20 minutes or more until apples turn soft, stirring halfway.
5. Serve straight away.

Chocolate Strawberry Shake

PREPARATION TIME
5'

COOK TIME
0'

SERVING
2

NUTRITION

Calories: 208
Fat: 0.2g
Protein: 12.4g
Carbs: 26.2g
Fiber: 1.4g

INGREDIENTS

2 cups almond milk, unsweetened
4 bananas, peeled, frozen
4 tablespoons cocoa powder
2 cups strawberries, frozen

DIRECTIONS

1. Place all the ingredients into the jar of a high-speed food processor or blender in the order stated in the ingredients list, and then cover it with the lid.
2. Pulse for 1 minute until smooth and then serve.

Chocolate Clusters

INGREDIENTS

1 cup chopped dark chocolate, vegan
1 cup cashews, roasted
1 teaspoon sea salt flakes

PREPARATION TIME
15'

COOK TIME
0'

SERVING
12

NUTRITION

Calories: 79.4
Fat: 6.6g
Protein: 1g
Carbs: 5.8g
Fiber: 1.1g

DIRECTIONS

1. Take a large baking sheet, line it with wax paper and then set aside until required.
2. Take a medium bowl, place chocolate in it and then microwave for 1 minute.
3. Stir the chocolate and then continue microwaving it at 1 minute intervals until chocolate melts completely, stirring at every interval.
4. When melted, stir the chocolate to bring it to 90°F and then stir in cashews.
5. Scoop the walnut-chocolate mixture on the prepared baking sheet, ½ tablespoon per cluster, and then sprinkle with sea salt.
6. Let the clusters stand at room temperature until harden and then serve.

Banana Coconut Cookies

INGREDIENTS

1 (½) cups shredded coconut, unsweetened
1 cup mashed banana

PREPARATION TIME
40'

COOK TIME
0'

SERVING
8

NUTRITION

Calories: 51
Fat: 3g
Protein: 0.2g
Carbs: 4g
Fiber: 1g

DIRECTIONS

1. Switch on the oven, then set it to 350°F and let it preheat.
2. Take a medium bowl, place the mashed banana in it and then stir in coconut until well combined.
3. Take a large baking sheet, line it with a parchment sheet and then scoop the prepared mixture on it, 2 tablespoons of mixture per cookie.
4. Place the baking sheet into the refrigerator and then let it cool for 30 minutes or more until harden.
5. Serve straight away.

Chocolate Pots

INGREDIENTS

6 ounces chocolate, unsweetened
1 cup Medjool dates, pitted
1 (¾) cups almond milk, unsweetened

PREPARATION TIME
4H 10'

COOK TIME
3'

SERVING
4

NUTRITION

Calories: 321
Fat: 19g
Protein: 6g
Carbs: 34g
Fiber: 4g

DIRECTIONS

1. Cut the chocolate into small pieces, place them in a heatproof bowl and then microwave for 2 to 3 minutes until completely melted, stirring every minute.
2. Place dates in a blender, pour in the milk and then pulse until smooth.
3. Add chocolate into the blender and then pulse until combined.
4. Divide the mixture into the small mason jars, and then let them rest for 4 hours until set.
5. Serve straight away.

Maple Syrup and Tahini Fudge

PREPARATION TIME
2 HOURS

COOK TIME
3'

SERVING
15

NUTRITION

Calories: 110.7
Fat: 5.3g
Protein: 2.2g
Carbs: 15.1g
Fiber: 1.6g

INGREDIENTS

1 cup dark chocolate chips, vegan
¼ cup maple syrup
½ cup tahini

DIRECTIONS

1. Take a heatproof bowl, place chocolate chips in it and then microwave for 2 to 3 minutes until melt completely, stirring every minute.
2. When melted, remove the chocolate bowl from the microwave and then whisk in maple syrup and tahini until smooth.
3. Take a 4 x 8-inch baking dish, line it with wax paper, spoon the chocolate mixture in it and then press it into the baking dish.
4. Cover with another sheet with wax paper, press it down until smooth, and then let the fudge rest for 1 hour in the freezer until set.
5. Then cut the fudge into 15 squares and serve.

CREASELESS

INGREDIENTS

3 tablespoons agave syrup
1 cup coconut milk, unsweetened
½ teaspoon vanilla extract, unsweetened
1 cup of orange juice

PREPARATION TIME
5'

COOK TIME
0'

SERVING
5

NUTRITION

Calories: 152
Fat: 10g
Protein: 1g
Carbs: 16g
Fiber: 1g

DIRECTIONS

1. Place all the ingredients in a food processor or blender and then pulse until combined.
2. Pour the mixture into five molds of Popsicle pan, insert a stick into each mold and then let it freeze for a minimum of 4 hours until hard.
3. Serve when ready.

Peanut Butter, Nut and Fruit Cookies

PREPARATION TIME
30'

COOK TIME
0'

SERVING
25

NUTRITION

Calories: 140
Fat: 7g
Protein: 3g
Carbs: 18g
Fiber: 5g

INGREDIENTS

¾ cup rolled oats
¼ cup chopped peanuts
½ cup coconut flakes, unsweetened
¼ cup and 2 tablespoons chopped cranberries, dried
¼ cup sliced almonds
¼ cup and 2 tablespoons raisins
¼ cup maple syrup
¾ cup peanut butter

DIRECTIONS

1. Take a baking sheet, line it with wax paper and then set it aside until required.
2. Take a large bowl, place oats, peanuts, almonds and coconut flakes in it, add ¼ cup each of cranberries and raisins, and then stir until combined.
3. Add maple syrup and peanut butter, stir until well combined and then scoop the mixture on the prepared baking sheet with some distance between them.
4. Flatten each scoop of cookie mixture slightly, press the remaining cranberries and raisins into each cookie and then let it chill for 20 minutes until firm.
5. Serve straight away.

Chocolate Covered Dates

PREPARATION TIME
10'

COOK TIME
3'

SERVING
8

NUTRITION

Calories: 179
Fat: 7.7g
Protein: 3g
Carbs: 28.5g
Fiber: 3g

INGREDIENTS

16 Medjool dates, pitted
½ teaspoon of sea salt
¾ cup almonds
1 teaspoon coconut oil
8 ounces chocolate chips, vegan

DIRECTIONS

1. Take a medium baking sheet, line it with parchment paper and then set aside until required.
2. Place an almond into the pit of each date and then wrap the date tightly around it.
3. Place chocolate chips in a heatproof bowl, add oil and then microwave for 2 to 3 minutes until chocolate melts, stirring every minute.
4. Working on one date at a time, dip each date into the chocolate mixture and then place it onto the prepared baking sheet.
5. Sprinkle salt over the prepared dates and then let them rest in the refrigerator for 1 hour until chocolate is firm.
6. Serve straight away.

Vanilla Hot Chocolate

INGREDIENTS

1/4 cup of cocoa powder
1/8 teaspoon salt
1/2 teaspoon vanilla extract, unsweetened
1/4 cup of coconut sugar
3 cups almond milk, unsweetened

PREPARATION TIME
5'

COOK TIME
10'

SERVING
4

NUTRITION

Calories: 137
Fat: 3g
Protein: 6g
Carbs: 21g
Fiber: 2g

DIRECTIONS

1. Take a medium saucepan, add salt, sugar, vanilla extract and cocoa powder in it, whisk until combined and then whisk in milk.
2. Place the pan over medium-high heat and then bring the milk mixture to a simmer and turn hot, continue whisking.
3. Divide the hot chocolate evenly into four mugs and then serve.

Vanilla Cupcakes

PREPARATION TIME
10'

COOK TIME
20'

SERVING
18

NUTRITION

Calories: 152.4
Fat: 6.4g
Protein: 1.5g
Carbs: 22.6g
Fiber: 0.5g

INGREDIENTS

2 cups white whole-wheat flour
1 cup of coconut sugar
½ teaspoon salt
2 teaspoons baking powder
1 (¼) teaspoons vanilla extract, unsweetened
½ teaspoon baking soda
1 tablespoon apple cider vinegar
½ cup coconut oil, melted
1 (½) cups almond milk, unsweetened

DIRECTIONS

1. Switch on the oven, then set it to 350°F and then let it preheat.
2. Meanwhile, take a medium bowl, place vinegar in it, stir in milk and then let it stand for 5 minutes until curdled.
3. Take a large bowl, place flour in it, add salt, baking soda, baking powder and sugar, and then stir until mixed.
4. Take a separate large bowl, pour in curdled milk mixture, add vanilla and coconut oil and then whisk until combined.
5. Whisk almond milk mixture into the flour mixture until smooth and the batter comes together, and then spoon the mixture into two 12-cups muffin pans lined with muffin cups.
6. Bake the muffins for 15 to 20 minutes until firm and the top turn golden brown, and then let them cool on the wire rack completely.
7. Serve straight away.

Conclusion

I am sure you have already started cooking away with some recipes, or if you haven't, you must be anxious to begin. You now have a wealth of knowledge on the topic of plant-based eating and hopefully, you understand the difference between all the various types of diets that fall under the plant-based eating umbrella. Use these various diets as stepping stones to reach the WFPB diet to gain all the health benefits from eating this way. Do not be guilty of not being able to change your diet overnight. Despite some people claiming it is easy to do this, in reality, it isn't the case for a lot of people. Maybe you are one of those who can and then I would expect you to be following one of the meal plans already, but if you are not able to make the switch (which I wasn't either), then go easy on yourself. Be merciful if you go back to your deep-rooted eating ways since it is something you have been brought up learning on so many platforms to be the "normal" way of eating, it's not easy to change your habits all of a sudden. When you fall back on those old eating patterns, just start again the next day and set smaller goals, one healthy plant-based meal a week is enough to start with. Soon you will be enjoying meat-free days, and then possibly meat-free weeks. This diet will take time to adapt to, but don't believe the myths you hear about this diet. You have seen the evidence in this book and you can always go further to look up the readings of Dr. Esselstyn, Dr. Campbell, Dr. Gundry and Dr. Greger. There is a lot of science-backed evidence for you to lean back on and motivate yourself with.

The abundance of benefits should be enough to get you started. Then the reduction of your risk of heart disease and diabetes will surely have you ready to continue on this new healthy eating journey. However, it may be the prospect of more energy, a slimmer waistline and a general feeling of good health that gets you going and not stopping. Either way, you are ready to begin and make the change. I hope you will use the extensive tips laid out in this book to keep your transition as smooth as possible and if you don't remember many of these, be sure to at least remember to increase your fluid intake to ease the digestion of all the fiber you will be enjoying.

Don't forget to stay away from unhealthy foods and soon you won't need to practice self-restraint to stay away, you will begin to stop enjoying those foods once your body is feeling the positive effects of healthy plant-based foods. Your body will change and begin to crave healthy sugars, fats and oils instead of fast foods and added junk in packaged food. You may still enjoy these as treats from time to time, and remember that is completely okay, but don't let it become a bad habit again, and if it does, just get back on track, and soon you will be back to where you were.

Start off by making the small substitutions of plant-based products over the traditional animal products such as cow's milk to soy or almond milk and then move on to the harder swaps such as from cheese to blended cashews and nutritional yeast. Also, be sure to avoid the common mistakes so many people have made before you. You don't need to go down these roads because other people, including myself, have gone down them already and we know what is at the end. However, if you do end up making one of these mistakes, don't feel bad, as I said, so many of us have done the same thing. One of the most significant takeaways from this book should be the guide on how to meet your nutritional needs, consult an expert on this to check your levels and don't think supplements are bad, they are necessary for those few nutrients we can't get from our food, on both an animal-based and a plant-based diet. I hope you will be able to avoid any discomforts from lectins and use the methods to reduce the unwanted side effects.

Manufactured by Amazon.ca
Bolton, ON